T0355148

Moral Progress

THE MUNICH LECTURES IN ETHICS

The Munich Lectures in Ethics series presents biennial lectures delivered by prominent philosophers at the Ludwig Maximilian University (LMU) in order to make their ideas accessible to a wider audience. The lectures are hosted by the Munich Center for Ethics, and they are edited as a series by Monika Betzler, who holds the Chair for Practical Philosophy and Ethics at LMU.

VOLUMES PUBLISHED IN THE SERIES

Philip Kitcher, *Moral Progress*

With Commentaries by Amia Srinivasan, Susan Neiman, and Rahel Jaeggi

Edited and Introduced by Jan-Christoph Heilinger

Moral Progress

PHILIP KITCHER

With Commentaries by
AMIA SRINIVASAN
SUSAN NEIMAN
RAHEL JAEGGI

Edited and Introduced by
JAN-CHRISTOPH HEILINGER

OXFORD
UNIVERSITY PRESS

OXFORD
UNIVERSITY PRESS

Oxford University Press is a department of the University of Oxford. It furthers
the University's objective of excellence in research, scholarship, and education
by publishing worldwide. Oxford is a registered trade mark of Oxford University
Press in the UK and certain other countries.

Published in the United States of America by Oxford University Press
198 Madison Avenue, New York, NY 10016, United States of America.

Library of Congress Cataloging-in-Publication Data
Names: Kitcher, Philip, 1947– author. | Heilinger, Jan-Christoph, editor.
Title: Moral progress / Philip Kitcher ; with commentaries by Amia Srinivasan,
Susan Neiman, Rahel Jaeggi ; edited and introduced by Jan-Christoph Heilinger.
Description: New York : Oxford University Press, 2021. |
Series: Munich lectures in ethics | Includes bibliographical references and index.
Identifiers: LCCN 2020055362 (print) | LCCN 2020055363 (ebook) |
ISBN 9780197549155 (hb) | ISBN 9780197549179 (epub)
Subjects: LCSH: Ethics, Evolutionary. | Ethics—Methodology. | Pragmatism.
Classification: LCC BJ1311 .K535 2021 (print) | LCC BJ1311 (ebook) |
DDC 171/.7—dc23
LC record available at https://lccn.loc.gov/2020055362
LC ebook record available at https://lccn.loc.gov/2020055363

DOI: 10.1093/oso/9780197549155.001.0001

3 5 7 9 8 6 4

Printed by Integrated Books International, United States of America

For Leo and Eva
with love

Contents

Series Editor Foreword   ix
Author's Preface   xi
Contributors   xix

Introduction: Democratic Contractualism: Philip Kitcher's
   Pragmatic Account of Moral Progress   1
   Jan-Christoph Heilinger

MORAL PROGRESS
Philip Kitcher

1. Method in Moral Inquiry   13

2. Problems of False Consciousness   41

3. The Many Modes of Moral Progress   73

COMMENTS

The Limits of Conversation   103
   Amia Srinivasan

Progress, Regress, and Power   111
   Susan Neiman

Progress as the Dynamics of Crisis   119
   Rahel Jaeggi

RESPONSE

Response to the Commentaries   139
   Philip Kitcher

Index   169

Series Editor Foreword

With the arrival of tens of thousands of refugees at Munich Central Station in the late summer of 2015, Munich found itself at the heart of one of the most profound challenges facing society today. The issue of migration was suddenly no longer remote and distant: answers to practical and often ethically complex questions were urgently needed. Of course, migration is just one of many challenges that this German city and the world are facing: climate change; the Covid-19 pandemic; digitalization and its impact on how we work, communicate, and lead relationships; and the development of CRISPR–Cas9 genome editing are no less pressing problems which require ethical reflection. Apart from such societal and technological changes, there are also many further ethical questions that confront us in our everyday lives. Is there such a thing as moral progress? Are human rights enough to address social and economic inequality? How can we capture and confront new societal injustices? What do we owe those with whom we have a close relationship? How can we provide ethical guidance on the area of aging? Can we go too far in the name of morality?

The aim of the Munich Lectures in Ethics is to address these morally relevant and pressing challenges, to advance our understanding of them, and to offer philosophically informed reflections and possible solutions to these issues. These lectures are held at the Munich Center for Ethics and Practical Philosophy, an interdisciplinary research center under the auspices of the Faculty of Philosophy of Ludwig Maximilian University (LMU) of Munich, the main goals of which are to enhance research in ethics and public debate on morally relevant themes and to foster collaboration with other subjects, most notably the sciences, medicine, business, and law. They thus contribute to creating a responsible research environment: they encourage individuals to be responsible actors and to work toward creating a more sustainable world. Located at LMU, one of Europe's leading academic and research institutions, the Munich Center for Ethics and Practical Philosophy is ideally placed to host the Munich Lectures, thereby helping to promote public debate on ethical themes of general interest and attracting the attention of a wide audience interested in ethically informed answers to the problems facing society today.

Inaugurated in 2019, the Munich Lectures in Ethics is a biennial lecture series, which takes place over the course of three days. Each of the lectures is followed by a comment given by a distinguished philosopher. The first lectures, which are published in this series, were delivered by Philip Kitcher, John Dewey Professor Emeritus of Philosophy at Columbia University, from June 5 to June 7, 2019, on the topic of "Moral Progress." Professor Rahel Jaeggi of the Humboldt University of Berlin; Dr. Susan Neiman, director of the Einstein Forum, Potsdam; and Professor Amia Srinivasan of St John's College, University of Oxford, commented on the lectures.

As the spokesperson of the Munich Center for Ethics and Practical Philosophy and as one of the initiators of the Munich Lectures in Ethics, I am extremely grateful to Philip Kitcher for having presented the first Munich Lectures in Ethics.

I am also indebted to Oxford University Press for having agreed to publish the Munich Lectures in Ethics as a series. These publications will make the lectures available to a broader international readership, thus giving philosophical scholarship the opportunity to influence matters of practical importance and provide much-needed orientation. I owe an enormous debt of gratitude to Peter Ohlin for his diligence and help with editing this series.

Monika Betzler
Ludwig Maximilian University of Munich

Author's Preface

Nearly a decade ago, in *Preludes to Pragmatism*, I expressed the hope that I should one day be able to provide a more systematic treatment of the pragmatist themes presented in that collection. As so often in philosophical explorations, eventual outcomes don't correspond exactly to anticipations. The present volume begins a partial fulfillment of my tentative promise. It will be the first of a trilogy, attempting to offer a more synthetic and unified account of ideas scattered among my earlier essays. Although each book is free-standing, they are intended to combine in developing a twenty-first-century version of Deweyan pragmatism.

Dewey insisted, throughout his mature writings, on the need for each generation to rethink the philosophical agenda in light of the circumstances of the age. I follow him in this. Hence this book, and its two successors, will attempt to reorient philosophical discussion by modifying the questions taken to be central. Central to philosophy, as I see it, is the concept of human progress. Like Dewey, I recognize the difficulties of that concept—and of making genuine progress—while emphasizing its importance. At the core of our shared vision is a sense of human lives and societies, extended over hundreds of thousands of years, in which each generation strives to improve the world it will bequeath to its successors. Nothing in Dewey's writings is more eloquent than the close of *A Common Faith*, where he writes: "Ours is the responsibility of conserving, transmitting, rectifying and expanding the heritage of values we have received that those who come after us may receive it more solid and secure, more widely accessible and more generously shared than we have received it." Here he specifies a general human task, one carried out in different ways by those who grow the food, make the artifacts, administer the laws, teach the young, heal the sick, engage in scientific research, offer entertainment and aesthetic delight, preserve the legacy of the past, sustain communities, foster peace and amity, and contribute in a host of other ways. Philosophy's peculiar duty is to try to make sense of the whole—to clarify, interpret, relate, and connect. In discharging this duty, it must seek to understand the progress made in different domains of human existence, and the unfortunate possibilities for interference ("institutional friction")— as when the drive for economic progress results in degradation of the environment, distorted educational programs, and the loss of community.

This short book focuses on one particular domain—moral life. It seeks an account of moral progress capable of helping individuals and societies fashion methods to make such progress more surely and more systematically. Of course, it seeks more than it delivers. What I claim to provide is a new approach to understanding moral progress, and some first steps toward characterizing a moral methodology. I see it as the beginning of a new—and more vital—way of addressing the uncertainties that give rise to moral philosophy.

My discussions here relate to work I have done before, most obviously to my earlier book, *The Ethical Project*. There I attempted to show how genuinely moral practices might grow out of pre-moral human life (to solve the problem of integrating ethics with evolution), to defend on this basis a naturalistic metaethics, and, as an afterthought, to mention some possible moral methods. In the present book, the emphases are quite different. The link to the evolutionary past is taken for granted, although I do outline a revised (and improved) account of the connection. Metaethics fades into the background. Center stage is occupied by the twin problems of understanding moral progress and moral methodology.

Change is naturally resisted. The most perceptive and probing questions I have received, from readers and audiences alike, have returned, predictably, to standard metaethics. Am I a peculiar type of moral realist? Is my position genuinely naturalistic? From my Deweyan perspective, those questions are (at best) secondary. The history of our moral progress has been chancy, blind, bloody, and constantly vulnerable to backslidings and reversals. Through an examination of that history, philosophy should seek to understand how to do better. If this book has anything important to say, it will lie in taking seriously the idea of method in moral practice, and in putting forward some preliminary—and surely *only* preliminary—suggestions for developing moral methodology.

Anyone who envisages turning an academic discussion in a new direction must acknowledge the possibility that it is all folly. At the times when I have wondered whether my orthodox interlocutors who (in kindness) want me to return to the proper issues of metaethics were right after all, I have been reassured by the reactions of some of my students. During my two decades of teaching at Columbia, one of its schools, the College of General Studies—often known as "the school of second chances"—has established a special place in undergraduate life. Under the guidance of an extraordinary dean, the late Peter Awn, it has attracted a wide range of students, whose varied backgrounds and whose diverse gifts have enriched our classroom discussions. Many of these students have grown up in hardship and have been deprived of significant educational opportunities; some are returning veterans; others have spent time in prison. When I have presented this material in classes, or have given my students early drafts to read, those who have been most embroiled in the hardships of the contemporary world have often told me how much they had been affected by my approach. "It speaks to me," they say, "in ways philosophy usually doesn't." Words like that have (maybe wrongly) encouraged me.

For, like Dewey, I firmly believe that philosophy should engage with the problems of life.

My debts to others are varied and numerous. First and foremost I want to thank Jan-Christoph Heilinger for his idea that I give the Munich Lectures in Ethics, for his splendid work in organizing the occasion, and for his warm support throughout my stay. Thanks also to Monika Betzler, who joined in issuing the invitation to me. I am also extremely grateful to Monika and the other members of the Centre, including the research assistants and the philosophical community at LMU, for their warm hospitality.

The lively intellectual atmosphere Jan and others have created at the Munich Center for Ethics was apparent in the quality of the discussions. Some of the points raised are duly credited in my footnotes. Many other people (whose names I unfortunately do not know) posed excellent questions, and I learned much from the unusually large number of comments and suggestions I received. They have had an impact on the material of this book and in shaping my future work.

My good fortune in having three brilliant philosophers as commentators is much appreciated. Some years ago, Amia Srinivasan's penetrating review of *The Ethical Project* prompted me to rethink the ways in which I had framed my proposals about moral life, leading me to focus more directly on moral methodology, and thus inspiring the approach taken in these lectures. I have been in dialogue with Susan Neiman for well over a decade, learning enormously from her deep knowledge of the Enlightenment and its legacy, as well as from her skill at connecting central philosophical ideas and theses to the problems of our times. For several years now, I have benefited from exchanges with Rahel Jaeggi, recognizing the intellectual kinship between our interests and some of our views, and benefiting from her insights as she develops kindred themes within a different tradition from my own. All three of my commentators are welcome reminders that deep, creative, and engaged philosophy remains possible today. I am grateful for their generosity of spirit and their constructive challenges.

It is entirely appropriate that my ideas about moral progress should have been presented in Germany, since that is the country in which they germinated and also where they have often grown. In 2011–2012, I enjoyed a fellowship at the *Wissenschaftskolleg* in Berlin, deliberately intending not to spend my time writing a book, but to read and think. My ruminations have led to my synthetic philosophical project—the elaboration of a Deweyan pragmatic naturalism for the twenty-first century. As anyone who has spent time at Wiko knows, the opportunities it provides are extraordinary. Besides the time to read and reflect, I was able to participate in a wide range of helpful discussions. Although my cohort of fellows was short on philosophers, I learned much from conversations, especially with Jeremy Adler, Alfred Brendel, Ayse Bugra, and Hollis Taylor.

In the autumn of 2015, I benefited greatly from another stay in Berlin, this time at the American Academy. Again, the support provided was superb, and I was able to develop my ideas further. Here, too, discussions were valuable, and I am indebted to Moishe Postone for helping me to overcome some of the limits of my methodological individualism; I suspect however that, were he still among us, he would continue to chide me gently. Three years later, in September 2018, I returned to Berlin to spend two months as a visiting senior scholar in Lorraine Daston's *Abteilung* of the *Max Planck Institut für Wissenschaftsgeschichte.* That enabled me to write the lectures out of which this book has grown. As always, I am profoundly grateful to Raine, not only for her warm friendship but also for our many conversations; for several decades, she has been among my very favorite interlocutors.

Another significant influence on my thinking about the issues discussed here has stemmed from my participation in the meetings of the Society for Progress. With the help of Michael Fuerstein, Subramanian Rangan has assembled an extraordinary group of economists, business leaders, and philosophers to consider the possible shape of a more progressive capitalism. I have learned much from our lively discussions, and from the contributions of David Autor, Julie Batillana, and Robert Frank, in particular. Amartya Sen has had a great impact on me, both through his writings and through conversations; I hope he will approve my expression of the opposition to teleology we share. Five philosophers—Elizabeth Anderson, Anthony Appiah, Michael Fuerstein, Susan Neiman, and Valerie Tiberius—have helped me greatly, in our discussions at the meetings, in their written work, and in a variety of conversations. Thanks to you all!

I have been extremely fortunate to spend the final years of my academic career in a wonderfully diverse, intellectually vibrant, and mutually supportive department. Several Columbia colleagues have helped me with the development of my thoughts about moral progress. I have learned much from Robert Gooding-Williams, Axel Honneth, Michele Moody-Adams, and Fred Neuhouser. It has been delightful and invigorating to recognize some of the affinities between my own pragmatism and critical theory as Axel practices it. Bob Gooding-Williams was extremely helpful in his suggestions for reading about the history of slavery and abolitionism; he has also generously provided me with excellent comments on a late draft of the lectures. Alice Kessler-Harris and Susan Pedersen offered me guidance in studying the history of the long movement for women's emancipation. I am also grateful to Tory Higgins for many conversations, and for the opportunity to read the manuscript of his book *Shared Reality,* in advance of its publication. To two distinguished economists—Ronald Findlay and Dan O'Flaherty—I owe a special debt; through our repeated ventures in joint teaching, my horizons have expanded and I have learned new ways of seeing.

For nearly forty years, I have benefited from regular exchanges with some exceptional graduate students. While these ideas were gestating I was particularly fortunate to be able to try out my embryonic thoughts on a group as talented as any I have ever taught. I am deeply grateful to Anuk Arudpragasam, Max Khan Hayward, Robbie Kubala, and Natalia Rogach Alexander for the many hours we have spent in conversations I have found not only valuable but also exhilarating.

Perhaps the greatest thanks are owed to a former member of the Columbia intellectual community to whom I can no longer express my gratitude. For nearly twenty years, Isaac Levi and I talked regularly. Although we were often in accord, we sometimes disagreed. I suspect (and hope) that Isaac enjoyed as much as I did our attempts to persuade one another. Unfortunately, he did not live to witness his greatest victory: my recognition that ontological debates are significant only insofar as they have methodological implications.

Besides presenting this material in Munich, I have been able to try out some of my ideas on other audiences. Early versions of parts of the lectures were presented as one of my Chaire Mercier Lectures at the Université de Louvain, at the Technical University of Delft, and in my visit to Berkeley as Howison Lecturer. Peter Verdée and Jeroen van der Hoeven raised many interesting questions (in Louvain and Delft, respectively). Discussions in Berkeley taught me much, and influenced especially Chapter 3. I would like to thank Shamik Dasgupta, Hannah Ginsborg, Wesley Holliday, Niko Kolodny, John MacFarlane, and Jay Wallace for their perceptive questions. John Campbell's comments on my Howison lecture have also prompted me to reconsider some aspects of my broader project. Finally, as ever, Barry Stroud offered me insightful advice; it saddens me to realize that I shall no longer be able to benefit from his wise counsel.

It has been, as always, a great pleasure to work with OUP's outstanding New York Philosophy Editor, Peter Ohlin. I am immensely grateful to Peter for his wise counsel and for his kind support.

At its best, philosophy is a cooperative enterprise. I want to thank all the people mentioned, and I apologize to anyone whom I have inadvertently forgotten.

And, of course, not least, I wish to thank Patricia Kitcher, who has influenced my thought (and my life) for nearly half a century.

Contributors

Jan-Christoph Heilinger is Researcher and Lecturer in Philosophy at RWTH Aachen University and permanent visiting professor at Ecole Normale Supérieure in Port-au-Prince. He works in moral and political philosophy with a particular interest in applied ethics.

Rahel Jaeggi is Professor of Practical Philosophy with an emphasis on Social and Political Philosophy and director of the Center for Humanities and Social Change Berlin at the Humboldt-Universität zu Berlin. Her research focuses on social philosophy, political philosophy, ethics, philosophical anthropology, social ontology, and critical theory.

Susan Neiman is Director of the Einstein Forum, Potsdam. Born in Atlanta, Georgia, Neiman studied philosophy at Harvard University and the Freie Universität Berlin, and was professor of philosophy at Yale and Tel Aviv University. Her research focuses on moral and political philosophy and the history of modern philosophy.

Amia Srinivasan is the Chichele Professor of Social and Political Theory at All Souls College, Oxford. She writes on epistemology, metaphilosophy, political philosophy, and the history and theory of feminism. She is a contributing editor of the *London Review of Books*.

Moral Progress

Introduction

Democratic Contractualism: Philip Kitcher's Pragmatic Account of Moral Progress

Jan-Christoph Heilinger

The present small volume contains a large project: Based on the assumption that a better understanding of past instances of progressive
moral change is crucial for making urgently needed current and future
advances in morality "more systematic and more sure-footed," Philip
Kitcher develops a novel understanding of moral progress as change
in belief and conduct, change that solves problems and overcomes
limitations in living together. Kitcher analyzes the dynamics of progressive change, including its main impediments, and proposes a
complex methodology of moral inquiry, guiding how individuals
and communities should go about realizing more such progress.
Challenged by constructive criticism from Amia Srinivasan, Rahel
Jaeggi, and Susan Neiman, also included in the present volume, Kitcher
concludes with a spirited defense of his vision of a society shaped by
institutions that invite and promote progressive change.

The discussions on moral progress are part of Kitcher's ambitious
project of a "reconstruction of philosophy" in a pragmatist spirit
that he has initiated in a number of articles, several of which can be
found in the collection *Preludes to Pragmatism*.[1] Furthermore, his

---

[1] Philip Kitcher, *Preludes to Pragmatism: Toward a Reconstruction of Philosophy*
(Oxford: Oxford University Press, 2012). The subtitle is an obvious acknowledgment of John Dewey's *Reconstruction in Philosophy* (*The Middle Works*, Volume 12,
1920 [Carbondale: Southern Illinois University Press, 1982]). Here Dewey argued for
redirecting philosophical attention from the perennial philosophical questions and the
quest to identify eternal truths, and to connect instead with the realities of human life
and address the challenges that currently emerge (cf. also John Dewey, *The Quest for*

Jan-Christoph Heilinger, *Introduction* In: *Moral Progress*. Edited by: Jan-Christoph Heilinger, Oxford
University Press. © Oxford University Press 2021. DOI: 10.1093/oso/9780197549155.003.0001

important book, *The Ethical Project*, has further set the scene with a
first presentation of "pragmatic naturalism" to approach questions of
moral philosophy with implications for adjacent social and political
philosophy: ethics and the moral rules that guide human actions and
interactions are to be understood as a human invention, a social technology developed to confront problems in living together.[2] Revisiting
these themes in the present book, Kitcher advances and enriches his
earlier work in different ways. If the preludes are over now, the present
book, the first in a planned series of three, could be seen as the first
movement of a full symphony.[3]

Starting from a phenomenologically careful analysis of past
instances of progressive moral change—the abolition of chattel slavery,
the expansion of opportunities for women, and increasing respect for
loving relationships between people of the same sex—Kitcher covers a
wide philosophical terrain: he touches upon the development of morality as a social technology over time; offers a pragmatic answer to
the metaethical question about the nature of moral truth; develops in
detail a method to pursue moral inquiry; and describes how such a
methodology could be practically implemented in society to seek and
realize progressive change.

In doing so, Kitcher aspires to work toward a "twenty-first-century
version of Deweyan pragmatism." In the following pages, this aspi-
ration culminates in nothing less than a first outline of a "Deweyan"
society. Such a society would harbor a distinctive "new cluster of social institutions" to address the current and future appearances of the
moral "ur-problem," which, according to Kitcher, consists in the limited psychological ability of humans to genuinely understand the perspective of others and to then shape their actions in the light of this
understanding. A (qualified) optimist by nature, Kitcher argues that

Certainty, in *The Later Works*, Volume 4: 1929 [Carbondale, Southern Illinois Press,
1984], 204).

[2] Philip Kitcher, *The Ethical Project* (Cambridge, MA: Harvard University Press,
2011), 3, 221, et passim.
[3] The other two, to be expected soon, will complement the work on ethics by a discussion of education, on the one hand, and of philosophy of science and value theory, on
the other.

intelligent interventions and reform, to which also philosophy can and should contribute, can trigger an entire "virtuous spiral" so that seizing some opportunities to realize progress can become increasingly transformative. In this short introduction, I offer some initial orientation to readers by highlighting three important dimensions of Kitcher's rich study on moral progress.

1. Moral Truth, Progress, and Methodology

The question about moral truth and the reality of moral facts and properties in the world has dominated metaethical debates for millennia. Moral progress, on the influential realist account, is understood as the discovery of objective truths leading to an ongoing epistemic approximation of full moral knowledge. Kitcher rejects this view and proposes, as a pragmatic alternative to a realist understanding of progress, to redirect philosophical attention: instead of looking for timeless, mind-independent objective moral truths, philosophy should aspire to identify problems that occur in living together and to propose intelligent solutions for addressing them. Insight in moral truth lies, on this pragmatist understanding, not at the origin of moral progress. Instead, progressive change in moral beliefs and practice allows that some novel moral commitments will be called "true," if they are able to lastingly convince people they are appropriate solutions to some perceived challenges in living together.

On this account, moral progress consists in a community progressing *from* a problematic situation to a novel arrangement in which the problem is adequately addressed, even though other problems might persist or novel challenges might appear. It does not consist in the claim of humankind altogether progressing *toward* some fixed end point of perfect morality. By acknowledging the complexity of the many dimensions of human social life, Kitcher's pragmatic account of moral progress saves the notion from the charge of being overly simplistic and too general, which has led to talk of moral progress falling somewhat out of fashion since its heydays in the eighteenth and nineteenth centuries.

If solving problems now is at the heart of moral progress, seeking progress could benefit from a systematic and methodological approach to problems to inform and guide a careful, complex, inclusive, and multiperspectival assessment in order to identify and implement progressive change—a long-term project that is handed over from one generation to the next.

The method Kitcher proposes comprises eleven steps and shows structural similarities with Dewey's pattern or method of (scientific) inquiry.[4] Dewey himself never explicitly suggested using his method to address moral problems, so Kitcher's methodological proposal can be understood as an original extension and elaboration of Dewey's method for the moral context. Both agree that, from an initially diffuse prima facie perception of an irritation or a problem, one has to move to identify and to precisely locate the problem. Next, several proposals for addressing the problematic situation need to be generated, discussed, and assessed in the light of the best available knowledge, and by taking into account and thoroughly engaging with the perspective of all affected others. Attempts to address the problem in practice are initially, inevitably, only of an experimental nature. One does not yet know whether the proposed change will solve the problem in an acceptable way. But if its implementation makes the problem disappear, the change can legitimately count as a solution (if not, alternative attempts to address the problem need to be undertaken); it can be called progress "if it would be retained in an indefinitely proceeding sequence of justified resolutions."

The methodology is the heart of what Kitcher calls "democratic contractualism," the ideal that ties justification—of diagnosis of a problem, of suggestion of a solution, and of resulting beliefs and action—to "a conversation in which diverse perspectives are represented, the best information is used [. . .] and in which all participants are committed to presumptive sympathy." A precondition for the successful deployment of the method, however, is a general willingness to do so which will only exist if an, at least basic, sense of

---

4 John Dewey, *Logic: The Theory of Inquiry*, in *The Later Works*, Volume 12, 1938 (Carbondale: Southern Illinois Press, 1986), 105–122.

community is already in place. Yet this often is not the case, as Kitcher acknowledges in his discussion of the impediments to moral progress.

2. The Moral Ur-Problem and Two Main Obstacles to Progress

Given Kitcher's acknowledgment of the complexities of human (moral) life, it may seem a bold move to identify a single "ur-problem" of morality at the origin of all morally problematic situations. But morality, which generally "focuses primarily on our interactions with others," has to come to terms with a particular challenge, namely the *limited human capacity of responsiveness to the plight of others*.[5] Responsiveness is the psychological ability to "tune [. . .] behavior so as to satisfy the desires of all affected better than would have been possible without the tuning."

The claim that such responsiveness is limited or restricted requires some explanation, since it includes two distinctive dimensions: there seems to be a natural limit to the amount of responsiveness humans can extend to the perspective of others. Our "native propensities for perspective-sharing are restricted," Kitcher writes, and cannot be stretched indefinitely. Yet under favorable circumstances—say, a general egalitarian commitment in society and freedom from immediate distress and competition—the potential of responsiveness could at least be fully exhausted. Yet it is a second type of limitation as impediment to progress, cultural not native, that particularly attracts Kitcher's attention: the dynamics of *exclusion* and of *false consciousness* constitute obstacles for progress because they make it difficult to even *perceive* a situation as problematic (i.e., problems go unperceived), when the psychological capacities of responding to the plight of others are not yet exhausted. Exclusion refers to the outright denial of moral equality by classifying humans in different groups, only some

---

[5] This claim is a significant development of Kitcher's earlier position, as presented in *The Ethical Project*, where he had identified "altruism failures" as the central moral problem. Replacing the narrower concept of "altruism failures" by the broader category of "limitations of responsiveness" allows capturing a larger and more relevant set of moral phenomena and problems.

of which are seen as having full moral status and thus worthy of equal moral concern. Racism, sexism, nationalism, and so on are the paradigmatic examples insofar as they deny some people full and equal membership in the morally relevant community. The second obstacle, false consciousness, is, according to Kitcher, an even harder problem, constituting a "formidable obstacle" to progress. Here, an entire community, including its oppressed or marginalized members, holds the belief that the status quo which so unequally distributes advantages in the community is *not* problematic: the disadvantaged have adapted their preferences to the limited range of options actually available to them, and all have acquiesced in the current unequal and unjustified distribution of advantages and disadvantages which are thought to mirror adequate assessments of the different capacities or natural roles of specific groups of people. Consequently no one, not even the disadvantaged themselves, perceives a problem and feels compelled to speak up.[6] Under conditions of false consciousness, engaging in an open and inclusive conversation among all affected will fail to identify moral problems, much less to deliver adequate reform.

These two obstacles need to be addressed if moral progress is to become less chancy and more sure-footed. With this intention, Kitcher's methodology for moral inquiry includes measures necessary to address them and to seek a joint "justified acceptance of a situation as problematic," overcoming conditions of exclusion and false consciousness. At the heart of the measures are periodic reviews of the status quo, independent of actual complaints or perceptions of a problem. These are held to question and assess whether the established and accepted rules and ideas that guide the self-understanding of people and their living together can actually be justified, or whether they

---

[6] For an another elaborate proposal to address the moral challenge of adaptive preferences, cf. also Serene J. Khader, *Adaptive Preferences and Women's Empowerment* (New York: Oxford University Press, 2011). Based on recent work on epistemic, particularly hermeneutical injustice, one might also want to add yet another impediment to moral progress that is a counterpart to Kitcher's explanation of the false consciousness of the disadvantaged: the oppressed might not speak up because they lack adequate concepts to understand, formulate, and express their perception of a problem (and not because they wouldn't harbor a diffuse feeling of a problem). In that case, overcoming the social restrictions that confine them is made even more difficult (Miranda Fricker, *Epistemic Injustice: Power and the Ethics of Knowing* [Oxford: Oxford University Press, 2007]).

unduly limit the opportunities of some. Deweyan social institutions, if implemented in society, would see to it that such questioning of the status quo is undertaken on a regular basis.

3. Democracy As a Way of Life: Individual and Institutional Progress

Kitcher explains in great detail the complex interplay between individual moral practice and social moral practice, the influence of the latter on the former (e.g., through model learning and education), and the dynamics of progressive change that can occur at both levels. Importantly, the method of moral inquiry is applicable to both dimensions: as individuals can face problematic situations, so can societies; and moral progress—in the sense of solving problems and overcoming limitations through modification of belief and of conduct—can be realized at both levels, leading to change not only in belief but also in corresponding conduct.

Too often, however, progress fails to materialize, for the reasons mentioned earlier. That is why the social moral practice in what Kitcher calls a "Deweyan society" will include a distinctive element that not only permits but actually actively invites and facilitates critical inquiry to identify and realize opportunities for progress. All societies have a moral code that permeates them in the form of certain beliefs, habits, and ways of talking. Furthermore, moral codes standardly include a number of unsettled questions, a methodology for moral decision-making and a specific form of social organization that reflects and supports enacting the moral code. A Deweyan society now would add a further dimension to the dimensions of social moral practice just mentioned, namely a "new cluster of social institutions" for critical inquiry and progressive change. Such an "institutional mechanism" would be the materialization of the conviction that societies, habits, and beliefs can improve further. The "mechanisms"—including the periodic reviews mentioned earlier—would be committed to democratic contractualism and thus call for a mutually engaging conversation between all affected, based on the best available information and executed in a cooperative spirit. And here, in spite of his elaborate skepticism toward presumed moral experts and special, individual moral authority, Kitcher even foresees a special role for philosophers, concretely for "Deweyan philosophers." These individuals, Kitcher contends carefully, "might emerge as particularly talented in identifying good topics for discussion, offering promising proposals for reform, and mediating the society-wide deliberations." Philosophy does not provide the answers, it has no special moral authority, but it has skills to facilitate moral inquiry and moral progress.

This vision of a Deweyan society, shaped by a radically enriched set of social institutions, concludes Kitcher's optimistic account of moral progress. It expresses the hope that a "virtuous spiral," triggered by instances of progressive change, might proceed "indefinitely in a progressive future whose characteristics nobody can currently predict."

Certainly, in the light of the grim realities of social inequality and deeply anchored structural injustice—locally, nationally, and globally—and in the light of an outright abuse of power or an inability to engage in a conversation, building one's hope for moral progress on conversation and a sophisticated philosophical methodology for moral inquiry might appear overly optimistic and utopian to some. All too often, some will abuse their power and block attempts to even start a conversation. When Philip Kitcher presented his manuscript in the form of three lectures on Moral Progress, all three commentators—Amia Srinivasan, Rahel Jaeggi, and Susan Neiman—challenged the optimism and the utopian character of Kitcher's account by stressing the role of power struggles, conflict, and crisis in advancing morality. Srinivasan additionally questions Kitcher's metaethical account and the presumed normative neutrality of his proposed method of moral inquiry. Neiman challenges the presumed central role of reason in making progress and doubts that genuine progress is possible without structural and systemic social change. Jaeggi also stresses the need to pay careful attention to the historical and socio-structural dimensions of progressive change, which often starts from conditions of crisis, and sometimes does not even start at all, when the time is not yet ripe.

The vivid discussions that were sparked by the thought-provoking comments included numerous aspects and suggested ways how to take Kitcher's proposal further. His reply to the comments, concluding the present volume, gives testimony to these discussions.

Kitcher's study hinges on the claim that "progress does exist," that progress has already occurred in the past, and that it thus remains a possibility also now and in the future. Certainly, past achievements are fragile and things can always also change for the worse. But beyond the need to defend what already has been achieved, the sheer possibility of progress is sufficient to justify taking up the challenge of seeking to realize more of it. Philip Kitcher's entire project of constructing a twenty-first-century version of Deweyan pragmatism—including its most recent building block, the present study on moral progress—is a call for societies and their members (with a particular focus on philosophers and those who are able to engage in critical and creative thinking) to accept their responsibility and to direct their skills and abilities to contribute to the project of making the world, for all those who inhabit it, a better place. In spite of the grim current realities and in spite of all the challenges that undoubtedly lie ahead, avoiding the task of shaping life together seems impossible, and resigning and remaining passive also seems not to be an acceptable option. Since progress is *possible*, it should be pursued and promoted with the best available means of human ingenuity, which, in the past, has already helped to remove barriers from human lives and to solve problems. The spirit that should prevail, and that permeates Kitcher's study on moral progress, is probably well captured in the words of John Dewey, who writes on the final page of "A Common Faith": "Ours is the responsibility of conserving, transmitting, rectifying and expanding the heritage of values we have received that those who come after us may receive it more solid and secure, more widely accessible and more generously shared than we have received it."[7]

---

[7] John Dewey, *A Common Faith*, in *The Later Works*, Volume 9: 1933–1934 (Carbondale: Southern Illinois University Press, 1986), 57–58.

MORAL PROGRESS

Philip Kitcher

1

Method in Moral Inquiry

I

At various stages in human history, particular societies appear to have
made moral progress. The advances often occur on several fronts.
There are public declarations, modifications of laws, and changes in
the attitudes as well as in the conduct of individual citizens. This diversity in the marks of progress is evident in the most commonly cited
exemplars: the abolition of slavery, the expansion of opportunities for
women, and the acceptance of loving relationships between people of
the same sex.[1] In the wake of change, older practices are frequently
denounced as barbaric. Young people who grow up under the new regime cannot understand why their ancestors were so blind and why
the shift in accepted morality took so long.

A closer look at the paradigms reveals that the advances were not
only slow; they also depended on events that might easily have gone
otherwise. Exceptional people emerged to speak with unusual clarity
and to display unusual courage. Quakers confessed their tender
consciences, slaves and ex-slaves shattered stereotypes of "the Negro

---

[1] These three cases will serve as my paradigms throughout. Others include the repudiation of honor killings (Anthony Appiah, *The Honor Code* [New York: W.W. Norton,
2010]), the increase of sensitivity toward animals (Peter Singer, *Animal Liberation*
[New York: Harper Collins, 1975]; *The Expanding Circle* [Princeton, NJ: Princeton
University Press, 2011]), and the evolution of the lex talionis (Philip Kitcher, *The Ethical
Project* [Cambridge, MA: Harvard University Press, 2011]). Perhaps most fundamental
are the extensions of moral protections already established for local bands to members
of neighboring groups. Such extensions must have occurred in the process of setting
up trading networks, which were in place at least fifteen thousand years before the
present. See Colin Renfrew and Stephen Shennan, *Ranking, Resource, and Exchange*
(Cambridge: Cambridge University Press, 1982), and, for the hypothesis that trade
in Africa developed significantly earlier, Sally McBrearty and Andrea Brooks, "The
Revolution That Wasn't: A New Interpretation of the Evolution of Modern Human
Behavior," *Journal of Human Evolution* 39 (2000): 453–563). The details are forever lost,
shrouded in the mists of the Upper Paleolithic.

Philip Kitcher, *Method in Moral Inquiry* In: *Moral Progress*. Edited by: Jan-Christoph Heilinger, Oxford
University Press. © Oxford University Press 2021. DOI: 10.1093/oso/9780197549155.003.0002

race," women sacrificed their lives to make a better world for their sisters and daughters, a small band of supposed "perverts" (as newspaper reports on the Stonewall uprising often dubbed them) defied the police in a Greenwich Village bar. Brave protests sparked social and political discussions, out of which new beliefs and practices emerged. It is all too easy to imagine daring checked by reasonable prudence, and a passive continuation of the status quo.

Optimists may suppose that, while fortunate happenings are required to initiate debate, they are followed by something less chancy—a discussion in which reason prevails. More realistic interpreters see contingency as playing a larger role. Luck is also required to keep the controversy going and to bring about the eventual change.[2] A moral revolution occurs because the social and political winds blow in favorable directions. Even when the revolution closes, old prejudices lurk uneradicated, and prior institutions are not thoroughly reformed. Structural racism and sexism persist; surface tolerance is given grudgingly and is accompanied by resentment of demands for "political correctness."

Moral progress does exist.[3] Yet it is chancier, slower, less thorough, and less systematic than it might be. One way of conceiving moral

---

[2] The movement to abolish chattel slavery in the United States depended on many events that might have gone differently. Even if the myriad alternative possibilities in the decades leading up to the American Civil War are ignored, emancipation of the slaves was by no means an inevitable outcome of that war. Most obviously, any of a number of battles turned on decisions and troop movements that were contrary to the judgments of the generals, so that the outcome could easily have been catastrophic for one of the armies involved. The Confederacy might well have obtained decisive victories, forcing the North to agree to secession. Alternatively, the Northern armies might have avoided the blunders that led to early severe setbacks, bringing about the original goal of the war—to restore the Union—before the abolition of slavery became an accepted extra aim (James McPherson, *Battle Cry of Freedom* [New York: Oxford University Press, 1988], Chapter 16, especially 490). Lincoln's bumpy route to championing emancipation, his abandonment of the idea of setting up a new and separate society for the ex-slaves, and his ability to win re-election were other loci of contingency (David Herbert Donald, *Lincoln* (New York: Simon & Schuster, 1995); see especially Chapters 13, 18, and 19). It is easy to assume in retrospect that the Northern states always aimed at abolishing slavery. In fact, throughout the entire period of the conflict, abolitionists constituted a minority, often viewed by fellow Unionists as extreme radicals.

[3] Many historians are—quite reasonably—opposed to casual celebrations of human progress. They view numerous announcements of progressive transitions as exercises in self-congratulation, typically ignorant of the complexities of the states before and after the supposed advance, and often linked to some indefensible teleology. I have tried to show how skepticism can be a valuable spur to making sense of the concept

philosophy identifies the function of the subject as that of supplying tools for facilitating moral progress. Dewey articulates this pragmatic conception. Judging history to show that human moral progress has mostly been blind, he proposes that greater understanding of moral progress will enable us to have more of it and to make advances "more intelligently."[4]

I share Dewey's hope. The aim of these lectures is to articulate a clearer account of moral progress than we currently have.

II

I expect many people (including many of my fellow philosophers) to endorse the goal of helping our moral progress to become more sure-footed—but as a spin-off from more central aims. A common description of the episodes with which I began would characterize them as involving the discovery of previously unrecognized moral truths.[5] Misguided attitudes give way to beliefs that correct previous errors or

of progress (in "On Progress," Chapter 7 of Subramanian Rangan, ed., *Performance and Progress* (New York: Oxford University Press, 2015); and "Social Progress," *Social Philosophy and Policy* 34, no. 2 (2017): 46–65). Of course, claiming that the notion of progress is coherent does not entail that humanity has made very much of it. Hence, I start from three examples, rather from any general thesis about the upward trajectory of our species. One of my paradigms, the abolition of slavery, has been hailed as progressive by two sensitive historians: W. E. H. Lecky, whose *History of European Morals from Augustus to Charlemagne* appeared in 1890, shortly after the demise of slavery in the Americas (reprinted edition; New York: George Braziller, 1955); and David Brion Davis, who recognizes the "fluidity" of the "connections between slavery and 'progress,'" but who also insists on not blurring the "crucial moral distinction" between enslaving and abolishing slavery (*Slavery and Human Progress* [New York: Oxford University Press, 1984], xix, xviii).

   [4] See John Dewey, *The Quest for Certainty*, in *The Later Works of John Dewey*, Volume 4 (Carbondale: University of Southern Illinois Press, 1977), Chapters 9 and 10; also "Progress," in *The Middle Works of John Dewey*, Volume 10 (Carbondale: University of Southern Illinois Press, 1977), 234–243.
   [5] This idea is by no means restricted to philosophers. It figures on the opening page of David Brion Davis's *Inhuman Bondage* (New York: Oxford University Press, 2008), a book rightly hailed as a brilliant study of the history of New World slavery: "The abolition of New World slavery depended in large measure on a major transformation in moral perception." The best exposition of the Discovery View that I know of is that offered by Thomas Nagel in "Moral Reality and Moral Progress" (currently an unpublished manuscript).

fill earlier lacunae. The *Discovery View* (to give it a name) identifies moral progress with a special kind of *cognitive* change.[6] Individual people make moral progress when they replace false moral beliefs with beliefs closer to the moral truth. Societies make moral progress when, in a sense to be explained, a similar process of replacing false beliefs with truer beliefs occurs in them. From the perspective of the Discovery View, Deweyan pragmatism starts in the wrong place, posing a derivative question and focusing on a derivative concept. What's needed is an account of moral truth, or a system of the moral truths, or maybe a method for finding the moral truths—a guide for the blind and perplexed. With that in hand, it will supposedly be straightforward to understand—and to make—moral progress.

The Discovery View (as I have so far formulated it) oversimplifies in two ways. First, in concentrating on psychological change, it allows transitions in which no alteration in actual behavior occurs to count as moral progress. Even worse, if the adoption of some new moral truths were accompanied by a sense of moral requirements as dauntingly demanding, thus sapping resolve to live up to them, an alleged example of moral progress might lead to a decline in conduct. Amending the view to avoid such implications is relatively easy. Discovery can be seen as *central* to moral progress, the source of wider changes in moral practice. My third lecture will explore some of the ramifications of this revision.

The second form of idealization consists in selecting a single judgment as central when moral progress occurs. Each of my paradigms is taken to involve some crucial recognition: slavery is wrong, women deserve greater opportunities than they have traditionally been allowed, same-sex love is sometimes virtuous and fulfilling. Anyone who studies the historical details quickly becomes aware of the many different ways in which these

---

[6] A related view might be defended by philosophers who adopt noncognitivism with respect to morality. They would regard moral progress as consisting in a different kind of psychological change, namely the replacement of feelings that are "less apt" with those that are "more apt." As my characterization suggests, an approach of this sort seems to be implicit in Allan Gibbard's *Wise Choices, Apt Feelings* (Cambridge, MA: Harvard University Press, 1992). For my purposes, this alternative is isomorphic to the Discovery View, since it presupposes a prior standard of aptness (the counterpart of a notion of moral truth). I shall henceforth simplify the discussion by focusing solely on the Discovery View, but I believe that my conclusions about it would apply equally to the noncognitivist relative.

generalizations are elaborated and linked to other ideas. Rejecting slavery is compatible with alternative visions of the rights to be enjoyed by those who have been freed and with greater or lesser departures from racial stereotypes. Similar questions are left open for the emancipated women, as well as for the gays and lesbians who are no longer regarded as disgusting sinners. Here, too, the Discovery View needs to retreat to emphasizing the centrality of some relatively imprecise new insight, and to explore the ways in which achieving that insight connects to other aspects of moral practice—including the social structures in which the behavior of individual people is embedded. Again, I defer the discussion.

Instead, I intend to proceed by leaving the view in its current, vague form. My principal aim is to contrast it with an alternative. Instead of viewing moral progress as a type of cognitive change, centered on modifications of belief to accord more closely with a prior, independent, standard, I suggest that individuals and societies make moral progress as they amend their moral practices to overcome the problems that beset them. Discovery of moral truth gives way to resolution of previous difficulties and expansion of previous limitations.

Stated so baldly, my envisaged rival will surely appear implausible. I can begin to motivate it by recalling a familiar fact. Many people, the Ivan Karamazovs of the actual world, distrust the notion of moral truth. A significant fraction of them embrace moral relativism, holding that we can only make sense of truth relative to something or other, not truth, period. Adherents of this view tend to think of moral progress as an illusion, typically conjured by the complacent in celebration of some contemporary ideology. When the relativists look at history, they see only a sequence of changes. Sometimes the changes go in a direction that later generations tend to like; at other times they yield far less welcome results. However they occur, there is no basis for singling out the favored ones as progressive. It is simply a matter of variable tastes.

The Discovery View responds to this skepticism by claiming that there *is* a basis. Some moral beliefs are objectively true; others are objectively false.[7] Of course, the view faces familiar challenges. What

---

[7] The view does not have to suppose that every moral question has an objectively correct answer. In some instances a moral proposition and its negation may both lack truth values.

makes the moral truths true? Some champions of the view would in-voke an abstract realm of moral properties; others would settle for something apparently more modest, claiming that there are facts about what people "have reason to do."[8] Both versions of moral realism have been subjected to further criticisms, on the grounds that they create an epistemological mystery about the relation between the realm of moral truths and the knowing subject, or even that no psychological capacity for detecting moral truth could have evolved.[9] My own concerns don't quite take either of the standard forms.[10] As I explore those episodes through which individuals and communities have changed their moral beliefs, apparently making moral progress, I'm deeply perplexed as to how what went on relates to any of the philosophical views of moral truth.

The trouble doesn't lie in any failure to understand what occurred during these transitions. Historians have written detailed con-vincing accounts of how slavery came to be rejected and how women's opportunities became expanded. Their explanations don't appeal to any philosophical view of moral truth, and they are none the worse for it. And that should be puzzling. For their colleagues who

---

[8] Derek Parfit (*On What Matters*, vol. 2 [Oxford: Oxford University Press, 2011]) opts for the former; the most prominent advocates of the latter ("non-Platonistic re-alism") are T. M. Scanlon (*Being Realistic about Reasons* [Oxford: Oxford University Press, 2014]) and Thomas Nagel (*The View from Nowhere* [New York: Oxford University Press, 1989]).

[9] A number of philosophers would view both styles of criticism as variations on a single theme, ultimately stemming from a line of argument developed by Paul Benacerraf in a very different context (see his seminal article "Mathematical Truth," *The Journal of Philosophy* 70 [1973]: 661–679). The evolutionary argument was originally formulated by Sharon Street ("A Darwinian Dilemma for Realist Theories of Value," *Philosophical Studies* 127 [2006]: 109–166), and it has been vigorously debated. For an assessment of the evolutionary considerations, see my "Evolution and Ethical Life" (in David Livingstone Smith, ed., *How Biology Shapes Philosophy* [Cambridge: Cambridge University Press, 2017], 184–203, especially 199–203).

Since Parfit's account is undeveloped—essentially amounting to a claim that the moral realm is "something I know not what" accessed "I know not how," the discussion in the text will concentrate on the considerably more plausible version of the moral re-alist position defended by Nagel and Scanlon.

[10] They are more closely connected with the epistemological worries (akin to those posed by Benacerraf in the mathematical case). I diverge in focusing more closely on how philosophical realism relates to historical explanations of changes in attitudes.

study episodes in which important new discoveries were made, the historians who recount how people became aware of genes or of black holes or of the relations among geological strata *do* have to explain how the discoverers were able to make contact with the entities whose properties were identified in the new claims. They have to explain—or at least presuppose—an account of how investigating the frequencies with which various types of pea plants are generated from crosses could enable Mendel to detect genes and to arrive at conclusions about some of their properties. How are we able to make sense of the recognition of new moral truth without some comparable story about the subject matter of morality, one that will reveal how those who changed their views about the legitimacy of slavery or the rights of women were able to achieve some comparable access? And why, when some account of the meaning and truth of moral statements is coupled with the historians' narratives, does it seem, not merely a weird and irrelevant add-on, but something that makes it mysterious how the psychological and social processes leading to the change could justify (or even generate) the new beliefs?

Metaphysically extravagant proposals (like Parfit's) generate the perplexity in straightforward ways. As we eavesdrop on the exchanges between opponents and defenders of slavery (say), what is it that the abolitionists do that enables them to track "moral reality"? How do their procedures differ from those of their benighted adversaries? Yet, even in the case of more modest forms of moral realism, similar puzzles arise. Those, like Scanlon and Nagel, who hypothesize objective facts about reasons, need to explain how a pioneering abolitionist— John Woolman, for example—was able to see that there are reasons for rejecting chattel slavery, while others, apparently with quite similar experiences and educational backgrounds, failed to do so. Many of those whom Woolman failed to convince were equally pious; they were thoughtful and kindly people who sincerely believed in the institution of slavery as beneficial to both races. How was Woolman able to see what they missed? What was the psychological difference between Woolman and the devout slaveholders with whom he debated? When exactly did the crucial recognition occur? And what justified Woolman in thinking that his reactions, including his opposition to the customs of his—godly—community, were correct? Those who argued with him surely saw themselves as reasonable people. What warranted Woolman's confidence that they were mistaken?[11]

An account of method in moral inquiry is needed, if moral realism is to be linked to the historical narrative. The mysteries would be dissolved if it became possible to see how the procedures conducive to moral discovery were followed by the participants on one side of an issue, and not by those on the other. The core of the relativist challenge is skepticism about settling moral disputes, a form of skepticism that would undermine talk of moral progress. The challenge can be met by providing a method for resolution. Without moral methodology, moral metaphysics is impotent.[12]

I hope the importance of this point will become clear as we proceed.

III

The difficulties with the Discovery View lead me to seek an alternative approach to moral progress. Instead of starting with a dubious concept of moral truth (or aptness of feelings), and then proceeding to the "ancillary" tasks needed to work out an account of moral progress, we might begin at the other end. Try to understand the notion of moral progress by specifying the relations obtaining when one practice gives way progressively to another. This venture is subject to two constraints. First, it must not involve any appeal to moral truth. Second, it must be integrable with the changes we theoretically cite as exemplars of moral progress[13]—rather than disrupting the narratives offered by historians,

---

[11] I have raised similar questions about realist approaches to mathematical truth in "Mathematical *Truth*?," Chapter 7 of my *Preludes to Pragmatism* (New York: Oxford University Press, 2012). The challenge, in both cases, is to explain how the view of "reality" relates to the psychological and social processes that occur in the historians' accounts.

[12] I am indebted to Isaac Levi for many years of exchanges about realism debates and for his insistence that, absent methodological implications, such debates are fruitless. Sadly, he did not live to see my public acknowledgment of this important insight.

[13] Might it not revise our opinions about some cases, leading us to see progress where we had previously overlooked it or to question whether something hitherto thought of as progress was the genuine article? Perhaps. The constraint is best understood in terms of the Carnapian notion of explication: although the explicated concept occasionally departs from prior usage, there must be broad conformity to older judgments. Moreover,

it should be at least consonant with them (and, ideally, should deepen the explanations they offer). In short, it should resolve the perplexities I associated with the prevalent accounts of moral truth.

If successful, this strategy might allow retrospectively for talk of moral discovery, and even see discovery in terms of the acquisition of truth. Moral discovery is simply what occurs when individuals or groups make moral progress. True moral judgments are those that result from moral progress. In William James's pithy phrase, "Truth *happens* to an idea."[14] More precisely, the moral truths are the judgments that emerge in moral progress and that remain stable parts of progressive moral practice, as it continues indefinitely. My third lecture will explore the promise—and the difficulties—of this form of pragmatism.

You might well think there's no hope of working out the details. For the idea of making sense of moral progress without relying on some cognitive or emotional achievement can easily seem absurd. The lack of a concept of true moral judgments or of apt moral feelings will doom any attempt to delimit the class of transitions in moral practice that count as progressive. It's a legitimate challenge. Let's see if it can be met.

IV

Progress concepts apply to many kinds of entities, or, as I shall call them, *systems*. People discuss the progress of the Catholic Church under different papacies, the progress of efforts to secure compliance to a particular law, or the progress made by someone learning to play a musical instrument. Behind these judgments stand (often tacit) ways of representing the state of the focal system and of partitioning the time interval through which progress is assessed. The progress of a firm is typically charted by considering the profits gained at regular intervals;

in light of the new, more precise, notion, we should be able to understand why we were mistaken in the particular deviations that occurred.

[14] William James, *Pragmatism* (Cambridge, MA: Harvard University Press, 1975), Lecture VI, 97.

the progress of the Church often divides time into unequal periods, corresponding to the various tenures of individual popes. Sometimes only one feature of the system, one *state variable*, is considered; those who audit the firm look only at a single figure (the profits). Frequently, several state variables are relevant; the aspiring musician isn't assessed on technique alone but also on sensitivity in interpretation.

When characterizing the state of the system under study requires attending to more than one variable, talk of progress can be stymied. Advances occur on one dimension, but they are offset by retreat along another, and there is no way to combine the gains and losses into an overall judgment. The changes occurring in the different state variables turn out to be *incommensurable*. To be sure, it remains possible to talk of progress and regress with respect to particular *aspects* of the system. But unqualified judgments of the kinds people often make are no longer available.

An important form of skepticism about talk of progress sees this predicament almost everywhere. The skeptic concedes the possibility of identifying progress in a few special cases. The progress of patients with high cholesterol levels or damaged hearts can be monitored by considering a single variable—the LDL concentration or the ejection fraction, say—and tracking its increase or decrease. When we discuss the important cases, however, the progress of humanity or societies or the moral progress of individuals, many variables come into play, and there are always gains and losses. Without any way of representing the fluctuations on a common scale, any overall assessment of progress becomes impossible.

The skeptical challenge contains an important insight. There are many hard cases, in which genuine incommensurability occurs. Moreover, many advocates of progress, people who trumpet the advances achieved by cities and economies and nations and the human species, frequently ignore some aspects of the systems they study, tac-itly assuming that their favored dimensions give a complete picture of the changes that have occurred. But does incommensurability always bedevil large-scale judgments of progress? I think not. Despite the absence of any general method for reducing different state variables to a common measure, it's sometimes possible to recognize that the magnitude of the gains achieved in one subset is clearly larger than the size of the losses incurred among the rest.

Consider the examples of moral progress with which I began. Whether you consider the abolition of slavery, the expansion of opportunities for women, or the recognition of loving relationships among members of the same sex, each case involves losses. Indeed, the valuable things given up in the transitions—the protective care furnished by benign slave owners, the devotion to nurturing the children without competition from external demands, the flourishing of a gay culture opposed to "normalization"—were emphasized, in each instance, by people who resisted the transition (or at least some facets of it). Calling attention to those losses can reasonably prompt efforts to re-establish, within the new framework, the values initially sacrificed. Yet it would be grotesque to judge them to be on a par with the advances that have occurred, or to think of them as compromising the progressiveness of the changes. Progressive changes occur in the sciences, although some valuable features of older practices are temporarily, even permanently, sacrificed. From the Bohr model to the puzzles of nonlocality, the physics of the past century has sometimes introduced incompatibilities with which researchers continue to struggle. They are rightly viewed as insignificant in comparison with the vast gains in predictive power, accuracy, and precision achieved in the progress of particle physics. Rather than undermining talk of progress, they point to opportunities for further progressive change. The same applies to the instances of moral progress I've taken as paradigms.

The skeptical fallacy is to infer from the incommensurability of some *changes* in different state variables to the incommensurability of the variables themselves. Despite the lack of any general method for reducing the different variables to a common measure, it is possible to rank some changes along particular dimensions as outweighing particular contrary changes along others. Once the fallacy is exposed, it's possible to understand how a concept of progress can be useful even though it fails to render a determinate judgment in all possible, or even in all actual, cases. Say that a progress concept is *global* if it generates a verdict in comparing any two states of the focal system. By contrast, a *local* progress concept offers a judgment about *some* pairs of temporally adjacent states of the system. The concept of moral progress I'll develop will be local.

Is that too little to ask for? Recall my Deweyan motivation for concern with moral progress. Understanding moral progress is to be the first step toward making our advances in morality more systematic and more sure-footed. To serve this purpose, many comparisons among states of individuals or of groups are irrelevant. Retrospective assessments, as with my paradigms, may help to test a proposed conception of moral progress, but, once a satisfactory account has emerged, its primary function is to assess potential ways of going on from where we are. Minimally, a local concept could discharge that function if it enabled us sometimes to identify a further progressive change, selecting one or more options of modifying the current state as instances of moral progress. More ambitiously, it might be *option-complete*, providing determinate judgments about each of the immediate changes in moral practice we envisage. If, in addition, it allowed for the comparison among any two of our potential choices, it would enable us to select an option at least as progressive as any other. The ideal would be a local concept, option-complete and option-comparative for all the circumstances in which we are likely to find ourselves. That ideal is almost certainly too much to hope for, but even a distant cousin, a much more limited concept allowing the assessment of some options in some contexts, would be worth having.

I've saved for the last the most important feature of my general approach to progress.[15] Many people think of progress as teleological: it

---

[15] A full account of progress concepts would have to explore another complication, one I take not to arise with respect to moral progress. Sometimes focusing on a particular system in isolation justifies conclusions about progress at odds with those that would be reached were the system to be set in relation to others. Progress judgments are relative to a *frame*, and modifying the frame can change the verdict. Consider a situation in which the focal system is an individual nation, its state taken broadly to include not only its economic condition and its political power but features of the lives of its citizens (indices of health, literacy, satisfaction, etc.). When the nation is examined in isolation, all the factors point to remarkable progress. In a broader frame, however, the nation is seen in relation to the sources of its wealth, particularly its exploitation of distant colonies, the lives of whose indigenous inhabitants are diminished by the uncomprehending rule of the colonizers and by the rapacity with which they consume natural resources and native labor. This phenomenon deserves more extensive discussion than I can offer here. I ignore it, because I don't see how anything of the sort can occur with respect to moral progress. The moral progress of one group doesn't retard, and may even advance, the moral progress of others.

is always progress toward a goal. Their paradigm is a particular kind of travel, in which the destination is specified in advance and progress consists in coming ever closer to it. Some types of progress accord with that model, but many do not. The aspiring pianist makes progress, although there is no Ideal Performer whose properties she successively approximates. Computer technology makes progress—the device on which I typed these words is an enormous advance on the bulky, limited, personal computers of the 1980s. Yet there is no Platonic Form of the personal computer, glimpsed by those who have emerged from the cave into the bright light of Silicon Valley.

Besides progress *to*, there is also progress *from*—*pragmatic* progress, as I shall call it. Both examples, that of the musician and that of computer technology, provide the obvious vocabulary for characterizing it. Pragmatic progress consists in solving problems and overcoming limitations: the pianist improves her technique by smoothing out her uneven trills and advances her interpretive sensitivity by understanding the structure of the pieces she plays; computer technology goes forward by correcting the current glitches and finding ways to perform tasks that were previously impossible. Stepwise pragmatic progress is guided by *local* goals. At each stage, the aim is to find relief from a problem or from a limitation felt as confinement. The break with teleology consists in the absence of any goal guiding the whole sequence of transitions. New problems emerge from the steps already taken to address older ones. How you go on depends on the decisions made in bringing you to your current place. To quote James again, "The trail of the human serpent is thus over everything."[16] At least, with everything associated with pragmatic progress.

So far I have only offered a framework, within which a pragmatist account of moral progress might be embedded. The next step is to identify moral progress as a local, pragmatic concept. That will require understanding the nature of moral problems and what might count as a solution to them. My casual talk of problems and solutions belies a serious difficulty. Is it possible to think of a situation as morally problematic without adverting to moral truth and falsehood? If the only

---

[16] James, *Pragmatism*, Lecture II, 37.

account of moral problems identifies them as predicaments in which some person, or some group, harbors false beliefs, my attempt to provide a rival to the Discovery View is plainly doomed. But what alternative is there?

V

In some domains, the notion of a problem is closely related to matters of truth and falsehood. The most obvious instances of scientific problems, for example, occur when the predictions made by the accepted lore of a field are at odds with the deliverances of experiment and/or observation. Elsewhere, however, particularly in practical matters, problematic predicaments have little connection with false beliefs. Someone who suffers from sickle-cell disease encounters problems when oxygen becomes relatively scarce, as at high altitudes. Whether that person's (or anyone else's) beliefs are correct or mistaken is utterly irrelevant.

Many people who have suffered from the crises of sickle-cell anemia have been entirely ignorant of what their problem is. Indeed, until the middle of the twentieth century, *nobody* could have provided a precise and accurate characterization of the trouble. So we must beware of supposing that to be a problem is to be recognized as a problem. Nonetheless, medical examples encourage a position I'll call the *Berkeleyan View*: a situation is problematic if those who find themselves in that situation seek relief from it. Problematic situations can be misunderstood, or the reaction to them can be confusion—something is wrong, and the sufferer cannot identify what it is. Hence one step in pragmatic progress consists in advancing from a problematic situation to a clear and accurate formulation of a problem. Desperate gasping for air gives way to attempts to relieve the blocking of the capillaries produced by abnormal hemoglobin.

Of course, on occasion people seek relief in cases where others see no grounds for doing so. The incorrigibly needy find problematic situations everywhere. If the Berkeleyan View were to see a problematic situation wherever anyone complains, it would be committed to an unacceptable form of subjectivism. There would be no problematic situations *simpliciter*, merely problematic situations for particular individuals, in greater abundance for the thin-skinned and scarcer among the stoical. But, as I have formulated it, the verdict of those with most fortitude is decisive. The problematic situations are those such that *anyone* placed in the pertinent circumstances would seek relief. The view could be articulated more circumspectly by thinking of an *objectivity spectrum*. At the subjective pole are situations felt as problematic by only a single subject; the objective pole is occupied by the situations all people view as problematic. The relative objectivity of different situations is measured by the sizes of the sets of subjects who would seek relief from them.

Invoking an objectivity spectrum explicates familiar ways of talking. Sometimes we see the trouble as lying with the subject: "There's nothing objectively wrong here," we say, "*you* have a problem, and you need to be more resourceful (less sensitive, more mature etc.)." On other occasions, the difficulty is taken to lie with the situation in which someone finds herself. To live under certain climatic conditions (temperatures far below freezing, or in regions with no access to water) is objectively problematic. There are intermediate cases, in which circumstances are objectively problematic for particular kinds of people, who cannot alter that fact through any change of attitude. Unlucky bearers of the sickling allele gasp for breath in environments that cause no difficulty for their more fortunate fellows; public buildings without elevators pose problems for those who use wheelchairs.

Yet, even with respect to medical problems, my elaboration of the Berkeleyan approach is unsustainable. Its bias in favor of the stoics is unwarranted. Their judgments aren't immune from error. Perhaps the well-trained Spartan with the dangling entrails doesn't take himself to have a problem, but he still needs surgery. And beyond the Spartans are people who take pleasure in experiences most people find excruciating, those for whom bondage and torture are preconditions of sexual fulfillment. The Berkeleyan View is a misguided attempt to elaborate a more plausible thesis, namely that situations are problematic when they are rightly judged to be problematic. It goes astray because, in identifying the right opinion with what is universally believed, it commits a familiar fallacy. Unanimity is neither necessary nor sufficient for correctness.

Indeed, the examples with which I began reveal the hopelessness of the Berkeleyan approach as a guide to *morally* problematic situations. For, as I immediately remarked about my guiding examples, slavery, limited roles for women, and the unnaturalness of homosexual relations were once widely accepted. Even if those views had been *universally* adopted, the situations in which they held sway should still count as objectively problematic. Given the aim of making moral progress more systematic and sure-footed, appealing to actual feelings as the touchstone for identifying moral problems is inadequate, precisely because of the importance of disclosing where change is needed, although the need is not yet recognized.

Unfortunately, this diagnosis reawakens the concern that the concept of a problem depends on some prior understanding of truth. For my critique of the Berkeleyan View referred casually to what is "rightly" or "correctly" judged as problematic. Have we then reached an impasse, in which no alternative to the moral Discovery View is available?

I think not. Despite its inadequacies, the Berkeleyan View, together with the medical examples motivating it, help us forward. They lead us to understand that what must be characterized is the concept of a problematic situation, a situation from which a defined problem may later emerge. Berkeleyans rightly see the problematic character of situations as related to human reactions to those situations. But they are too easy-going in resting with the *actual* reactions people express. What is needed is some account of when those reactions are *justified*. Behind the talk of "rightness" is not an illicit appeal to truth, but an as yet unexplicated notion of justification.

VI

Human beings are fallible. Sometimes we identify our circumstances as problematic when what requires amendment is our reaction to them. On other occasions we err in the opposite direction, failing to recognize the problematic character of the status quo. Moral progress would become more assured and less chancy if we had an ideal diagnostic tool, one that would show where the problems lie and where they don't. Demanding that much is unnecessary, however, and seeks something almost certainly beyond our powers. We could make progress with moral progress with considerably less, with some imperfect instruments, capable of improving the problem discriminations people actually make.

It's useful to begin with one of our potential errors, the one I originally used to motivate my inquiry. After the repudiation of slavery, the embrace of wider opportunities for women, and the acceptance of same-sex love, we can ask what our ancestors, whom we now see as mired in prejudices, were missing. Perhaps if we recognize the sources of their errors we shall be able to avoid making similar mistakes in the future, or, at least, our similar blunders will be less frequent. What kind of blindness occurred in those who viewed the enslavement of people with dark skin as entirely acceptable, in those who thought it appropriate to confine women to the domestic sphere, and in those who railed against same-sex relationships as disgusting and unnatural?

A preliminary question: How widespread was the blindness? That surely varies with place and period. Almost certainly, there have been occasions on which some of the people whose lives we now understand as confined by the moral blindness of the ambient society—the slaves, the women, those drawn to members of their own sex—felt that confinement. Even if outsiders failed to recognize the problematic features of their predicament, those who suffered under it understood. In such cases, the central question can be formulated more specifically: Why did the devotees of the prevailing moral order pay no heed to the awareness of oppression present in the oppressed? Here, we might say, there's an obvious failure of sympathy. Opinions voiced by people who suffer and who express their suffering are disregarded. Failure to take them seriously may rest on drawing a distinction among types of human beings, on supposing some members of our species to be unqualified on particular topics or even in taking them to be inferior altogether. Because of their deficiencies, these subjects have no place in a responsible moral discussion. Sympathy for them, and for their judgments on their lives, thus lapses.

In an unduly optimistic moment, William James identifies the predicament of the moral philosopher. The philosopher cannot recognize in advance the optimal moral organization of the universe. Instead, "he only knows that if he makes a bad mistake the cries of the wounded will soon inform him of that fact."[17] James's insight here is that moral philosophy advances on actual moral life by listening for the cries of the wounded. The optimism consists in failing to see that sometimes the wounded do not even cry.

Blindness (or, to follow James in switching to a different sensory modality, moral deafness) may spread more widely, being shared by the victims themselves. With respect to slavery, women's roles, and same-sex love, the judgments of the oppressors have sometimes—how frequently is unknown—shaped the attitudes of the oppressed. At various times and places, slaves have acquiesced in their bondage, women seen the domestic sphere as their natural place, and people attracted to their own sex experienced self-loathing as a consequence of their "perverted" tendencies. Even if the local guardians of morality had thought to ask members of the marginalized group, they would only have heard an echo of their own dominant views. Is there a failure of sympathy here? Imagine the kindly Victorian husband, seated across the fireplace from his devoted spouse, solicitously interrupting her needlework to inquire if she is really, truly, deeply happy with what he has provided for her—and her reply, gentle but firm, as she raises her adoring eyes to reassure and thank him. Does her response pay tribute to his genuine sympathy?

In my exemplars, problems go unperceived either as a result of *exclusion* or because of widespread *false consciousness*. My attempt to use the exemplars of moral progress to elaborate the concept of *justified acceptance of a situation as problematic* will treat these cases sequentially, beginning with the easier instance of exclusion. Before embarking on this venture, however, it is helpful to reflect a little on the Deweyan goal of rendering moral progress more systematic, more frequent, and more secure, so that it is clear how my strategy offers a *partial* advance toward that goal.

It would be obvious folly to regard all misjudgments about problematic situations as stemming from one of the two forms of blindness I have pointed to. Human fallibility comes in a large array of guises.

---

[17] William James, "The Moral Philosopher and the Moral Life," in *The Will to Believe and Other Essays* (Cambridge, MA: Harvard University Press, 1979), 158.

The search for improving our prospects of making moral progress has led to the question of understanding when situations are justifiably viewed as morally problematic—or, more exactly, of replacing current inchoate ideas with respect to that question with something more definite and more accurate. One obvious way to do so is to examine ways in which past indifference to morally problematic situations has manifested itself. Even if the examples that initially suggest themselves do not fully represent the wide range of ways in which our embryonic thoughts about what is morally problematic can lead us astray, they offer a place for beginning the project of improvement. With their aid, some useful directives for moral inquiry may emerge. Furthermore, when those directives are put to work, other related phenomena, currently not clearly discerned, may spring into focus, leading future investigators to a more encompassing account of what is justifiably taken to be morally problematic. First attempts to forge the Deweyan tools can lead to more adequate instruments and a fuller toolbox.

In an important essay—the best philosophical account of Darwin's significance written in the century following the publication of the *Origin of Species*—Dewey characterized Darwin's achievement in methodological terms.[18] The great pioneers of the seventeenth century, Galileo, Bacon, Descartes, Boyle, Newton, and others, had developed methods for investigating physical phenomena (particularly aspects of motion). Darwin extended the scope of methods of disciplined inquiry, so as to embrace the living world. His accomplishment set the stage for a further step: to elaborate methods for inquiry in the human and moral sciences. The goal, as Dewey recognizes, is to make progress in these domains less chancy than it has hitherto been.

Anyone who reflects on the historical episodes motivating Dewey's emphasis on method should draw some obvious conclusions. First, the search for a method involves addressing three questions: Where does one begin inquiry? How does one conduct inquiry? and How does one end inquiry? Different questions are prominent in different cases. One of Darwin's major methodological advances consists in his recognition

---

[18] Dewey, "The Influence of Darwin on Philosophy," in *The Middle Works of John Dewey*, Volume 4 (Carbondale: University of Southern Illinois Press, 1977), 3–14.

of questions worth asking.[19] Second, the initial attempts to formulate methodological proposals are notoriously vague and incomplete. The various dicta of Bacon, Descartes, Galileo, and others are hard to reconcile with one another, but they serve as inspiration for investigations in which they are used selectively and given more definite shape. Out of those particular inquiries, and attention to the record of successes and failures, superior formulations of the original maxims emerge. More precise directives generate new research, and methods continue to be refined. The histories of the sciences testify to something specialists take as a truism, but which is not broadly appreciated: methodology doesn't descend from some a priori heaven but is built up, in stages, out of fallible human explorations.

The same goes for moral inquiry and for moral progress. To advance the Deweyan goal of making our moral progress more surefooted, methods for moral inquiry are required. To develop such methods is to offer more definite proposals about how morally problematic situations might be identified, about how efforts to cope with what has been judged as problematic might be directed, and about the conditions under which those efforts should bring about moral change. The successes and failures of the past can help in fashioning such proposals. If we start with a small sample of "obvious" or "spectacular" examples, that is by no means to take the paradigms as fully representative. They simply provide a point of entry, intended to facilitate better moral inquiry out of which superior methodological advice may emerge. As with the physical and biological sciences, they begin a virtuous spiral, proceeding indefinitely in a progressive future whose characteristics nobody can currently predict. When we make progress with respect to nature or morality, we also learn more about how to make further progress.

---

[19] I develop this point in "Darwin's Achievement" (Chapter 3 of Philip Kitcher, *In Mendel's Mirror* [New York: Oxford University Press, 2003]) and in Chapter 2 of *The Advancement of Science* (New York: Oxford University Press, 1993). Einstein's famous characterization of his route to the special theory of relativity echoes the Darwinian focus on the starting points for inquiry. He describes himself as posing questions nobody had thought to ask. In *Einstein's Clocks, Poincaré's Maps* (New York: W.W. Norton, 2003), Peter Galison brilliantly scrutinizes Einstein's autobiographical claims.

These more general views of method, its importance, and its development should explain the strategy I have proposed. Through considering cases, first of exclusion, then of false consciousness, I hope to advance some proposals for improving moral inquiry. Let's now turn to assembling the clues history offers.

VII

Insofar as the problems with slavery, or with the confinement of women, or with the persecution of homosexuals, went unnoticed because of exclusion, the transitions from blindness to recognition display a common structure. Initially, the resentments of the oppressed are private. Victims experience distress and, at most, communicate their woes to one another. Attempts to protest what is done to them go unheard (at best) and frequently incite acts of discipline and punishment. One focal example can serve. In 1616, when the fourteen-year-old daughter of Sir Edward Coke, former Chief Justice of England, refused to marry the man of her father's choice—the psychologically disturbed brother of the Duke of Buckingham—Coke abducted her, tied her to a bedpost, and whipped her until she gave her consent.[20]

Each of the transitions is complex, interweaving processes in which exclusion is partially broken down, so that, in different times and places, different individuals and groups come to engage more fully with the emotions, opinions, and complaints of those whom they have previously judged to be incompetent (if not perverse) in the relevant sphere. The actual history also involves processes of a different kind, in which false consciousness plays a role. For the present, however, the latter will be ignored, in favor of concentrating on the simpler sequence of events, in which, in stages, the voices of the oppressed became more audible, and social opinion was shifted.

Neglecting all the perturbations, we can trace the arc as it bends away from injustice. Initially, some brave individual, either a member of the marginalized class or someone with unusual sympathy for that class,

---

[20] Lawrence Stone, *The Family, Sex, and Marriage in England, 1500–1800* (New York: Harper and Row, 1977), 182–183.

speaks out loudly enough to force the attention of a small group among the privileged. The speakers are always vilified and sometimes pay for their temerity with their lives. Their achievement consists in starting a public conversation. When it goes well, the conversation attracts more dissident voices and a wider circle of sympathetic listeners, so that later stages build on ground already conceded, shifts of opinion effected by earlier conversations. Of course, the initial discussion can fizzle out and even end in intensification of the old attitudes.

To the extent that exclusion plays a role in my chosen exemplars of moral progress, the historical course of change is slow, chancy, and wasteful—full of unnecessary delays, reversals, pain, and misery— because there is no automatic process of initiating conversation under circumstances in which subjects recognizably suffer under conditions that are currently permitted.[21] This conclusion provides a basis for refining the Berkeleyan View considered earlier.

1. A situation is prima facie morally problematic if there is some individual or group of individuals who resent the fact that the accepted moral framework permits it.

The justification for counting situations as problematic (period) emerges from moral inquiry. A first methodological maxim takes prima facie morally problematic situations as legitimate starting points for inquiry,[22] and moral inquiry as consisting in an *ideal conversation*.

2. If a situation is prima facie problematic, and if its problematic status is urgent, it should initiate moral inquiry.
3. Properly pursued moral inquiry initiated by a prima facie problematic situation consists in an ideal conversation appropriate to that situation.

---

[21] I have deliberately chosen an awkward phrasing here to allow for the possibility of initiating discussion in cases where the subjects in question (human beings unable to communicate with the pertinent audience or sentient nonhuman animals) cannot express their concerns. Although my formulations assume that the deliberators are human beings, I want to allow for the possibility of representing nonhuman animals. For more detailed discussion of how I envisage this, see my "Experimental Animals," *Philosophy and Public Affairs* 43 (2015): 287–311.

[22] Hence following James's directive to listen for the cries of the wounded.

In formulating these proposals, I've introduced an unexplained notion, that of the *urgency* of a problematic situation, and have characterized conversations as *appropriate* to situations. So clarification is required.

Human beings are not just fallible—our resources are also finite. Arguably, the number of situations in which people register complaints is so great as to prevent any effort to respond to all of them at once. Indeed, in each of the historical episodes I've considered, other lines of potential moral improvement competed with the calls for liberation of the courageous challengers I've mentioned.[23] Quite possibly *many* of the rival lines of moral inquiry might have led to moral and social reforms. Some clearly did, as in Elizabeth Fry's campaign for prison reform, which undermined the prior moral disposition to treat criminals as beyond important protections. The moral community might also have attended to less weighty complaints, listening to the pleas of the well-off for release from moral requirements they found irksome—challenges to the permissibility of various types of taxation, for example. Just as a scientific community can be criticized if it focuses its efforts on trivial questions—or on socially dangerous lines of research—so, too, with respect to moral inquiry. The court should take up cases in which the pleas are most urgent.

How is urgency to be judged? An obvious large danger is that the calls of the marginalized will be dismissed in favor of those expressed by people who currently sit comfortably within the moral framework. Slaves and "perverts" have no standing; women have standing only so long as they do not venture beyond their "proper place." The danger is manifest in some of the historical responses, in judgments condemning fruitless discussion of issues that are firmly settled. To ward off that skewing of moral inquiry, decisions about the urgency of a challenge should start with a provisional adoption of the extended sympathy moral inquiry might ultimately generate. Urgency, we might say, varies directly with the impact of the challenged practice and the

---

[23] With respect to slavery, issues about the treatment of workers in the nascent industrial revolution become salient (David Brion Davis, *Inhuman Bondage* [New York: Oxford University Press, 2008], 191–192). In nineteenth-century debates about opportunities for women, there are frequent connections to issues about the possibilities for the poor (Barbara Taylor, *Eve and the New Jerusalem* [Cambridge, MA: Harvard University Press, 1983]).

size of the group affected by it. There can be difficulties in deciding how to trade impact and group size against one another—as when people debate whether a moral burden imposed on a relatively small human population takes precedence over attending to currently tolerated conduct that causes suffering for a vast population of nonhuman animals. So I shall not offer a precise measure. Instead, I imagine justified assessments of urgency to result from a conversation in which diverse perspectives are represented, the best available information is used in estimating impact and group size, and in which all the participants are committed to presumptive sympathy with those who bring the challenge—that is, they deliberate as if that challenge were justified.

4. If a challenge is brought to members of a particular group, then it counts as urgent just in case a fully inclusive, optimally informed deliberation among representatives of the different perspectives within the group, committed to presumptive sympathy with the challengers, would endorse that challenge as one of the urgent candidates for moral inquiry.

5. A group's moral inquiries into challenges are justified just in case (i) each of the challenges investigated belongs to the set of urgent candidates, and (ii) there is no challenge selected for investigation such that some challenge not selected is unanimously ranked as more urgent by the deliberation through which the urgency of challenges is measured.

The maxims so far assembled allow a straightforward account of when prima facie problematic situations are justifiably taken to be problematic (period).

Justification emerges from the process of moral inquiry. A challenge is brought, its urgency is assessed, moral inquiry begins, and, after it has run its course, generates the judgment that a problem previously existed, unrecognized by some—perhaps by a vast majority—but now clearly visible. Hence:

6. A situation is justifiably taken to be problematic just in case a properly pursued moral inquiry initiated by that situation would generate the conclusion that it is indeed problematic.

Moral inquiry is properly pursued, I have suggested (see principle 3 earlier), when it takes the form of a particular kind of conversation. The dominant ideal here is democratic. Imagine a group of deliberators, including all those affected by the challenged practice and all those who would be affected if that practice were to be amended. Call these people *stakeholders*. The deliberation must be inclusive in the sense of including representatives of all the perspectives adopted by the stakeholders. One condition on being a conversation appropriate to a situation is that it be sufficiently inclusive. Another is that it rely only on the available set of justified information. The third such condition requires the participants to be mutually engaged: each of them is committed to seeking a proposal for responding to the situation with which the other deliberators are prepared to live. Combining these thoughts, we obtain:

7. An ideal conversation appropriate to a prima facie problematic situation is a discussion in which the perspectives of all the stakeholders (with respect to that situation) are represented, in which proposals for responding to the situation are only considered if they, and the judgments put forward in their support, are consistent with the best information available in that situation, and in which the participants are mutually engaged.

Together, 3, 6, and 7 yield the conclusion that a prima facie problematic situation would be endorsed as problematic just in case an ideal conversation meeting these conditions would endorse it as such. More simply, problematic situations are those that societies would view as problematic if representatives of all the various affected standpoints with respect to that situation would agree on its troublesome character if they were to deliberate together on the basis of the corpus of justified factual beliefs under conditions of deep mutual respect and sympathy.[24]

---

[24] The central role that a particular style of conversation plays in my proposed moral methodology links me to other "constructivist" ventures in moral philosophy. As I've suggested elsewhere, the emphasis on mutual engagement echoes some themes in Adam Smith's *Theory of Moral Sentiments* (see my essay, "The Hall of Mirrors," reprinted as Chapter 14 of *Preludes to Pragmatism*). There are also connections to the third formulation of the Categorical Imperative (the "ugly duckling" of Kant's *Groundwork*), to Rawls's

The next step is to explicate the concept of a justified resolution to a problematic situation. The obvious way to extend the approach I've outlined—henceforth *democratic contractualism*—would be to identify a proposal for amending moral practice as justified provided that it is endorsed by the participants in an ideal conversation. Here, however, a slight complication arises. It is possible for people not originally included among the stakeholders for the problematic situation to be affected by any implementation of the proposal. If that is so, their perspectives should also be represented in the discussion. Since the ultimate aim is to understand moral progress, and since progress talk compares two states, one governed by the original practice and one governed by the amended practice, the inclusiveness condition should encompass both those affected under the old regime and those affected under the proposed new one.

8. A proposal is a justified resolution of a problematic situation just in case the transition from the problematic situation to that proposed would be endorsed in an ideal conversation in which the perspectives of stakeholders with respect to both situations were represented.

The Deweyan goal of improving moral decision-making—rendering moral progress less chancy—involves finding practical means for doing the best we can to facilitate justified resolutions.

"Kantian Constructivism in Moral Theory" (*Journal of Philosophy* 77 [1980]: 515–572), and to the writings of Jürgen Habermas. To my mind, the principal differences between these approaches and my own are as follows: first, that Kant, Rawls, and Habermas all adopt the perspective of ideal theory, while I am concerned with historical situations that are far from ideal; and second, that, where they envisage general conditions on the decision-making of an idealized abstract individual, I am concerned with diverse individuals, with varying levels of knowledge, and with attempts at sympathetic mutual understanding. Perhaps the closest linkage is to T. M. Scanlon's *What We Owe to Each Other* (Cambridge, MA: Harvard University Press, 1998). Like others influenced by Kant, Scanlon's treatment abstracts from the concrete predicaments of individuals and societies, hypothesizing a general and historically invariant notion of reason (and of reasonableness). My endeavor can be viewed as an attempt to place "reason" within history and to provide methodological guidelines for its progressive development.

Notice, however, that an account of moral progress has not yet emerged. So far, I have offered a view about how we might be *justified*—prospectively or retrospectively—in judgments about moral progress. Yet, as I have reiterated, human judgments are fallible. Even when we think of ourselves as making moral progress, we may be wrong.

How could that be? Well-intentioned attempts to resolve problematic situations can founder for three major reasons. First, even though deliberators employ the best available information, the beliefs justified in their context, they may err: the proposal they endorse may be compatible with the current set of justified judgments, but not those endorsed in a factually superior practice (either because that practice revises some of the accepted judgments or because it accumulates new information, inconsistent with the proposal). Second, despite their attempts to achieve understandings of one another's positions and predicaments, they may fail. With the best intentions, those privileged under the status quo can fall short of comprehending the plight of the challengers, while those who have suffered may view sympathy as requiring them to accept some proposal that will not ameliorate their predicament. Third, the side effects of change are often unpredictable. Apparently well-grounded proposals for change may turn out to be impossible to live with.

Real progress occurs when justified progressive shifts endure. Imagine a moral community conforming to the methodological maxims 1–8. During its indefinitely extended career, challenges constantly arise, prompt moral inquiry, and are resolved. At each stage, the community does the best it can—by the lights of 1–8. Sometimes previously justified shifts are reversed or simply become irrelevant. Those instances contrast with the cases of genuine progress, marked by the indefinite retention of features of particular transitions. Progress happens when *justification sticks*.

9. A change in moral practice is progressive just in case it would be retained in an indefinitely proceeding sequence of justified resolutions.

I offer 1–9 as a preliminary proposal for a methodology of moral inquiry. As my remarks about the seventeenth-century ventures in the search for method indicate, it is overwhelmingly probable that any future attempts along these lines will look back on my maxims as crude, vague, and conceptually inadequate. The hope, however, is that they might initiate a program that will transcend them.

2

Problems of False Consciousness

I

In my first lecture, I used three instances of moral progress to motivate some methodological maxims for moral inquiry. My venture into moral methodology embodies the Deweyan hope of rendering future moral progress more systematic and sure-footed. So far, however, I have only dealt with one of the retarding factors evident in the historical episodes, the phenomenon of *exclusion* or *moral deafness*. If the difficulties that complicated and delayed moral progress are to be addressed, it will also be necessary to come to terms with the harder problem posed by false consciousness. To do that, I shall need to deepen my historical investigations. So I shall start by looking more closely at the relations between the maxims I have proposed and the historical examples, and also by considering the broader sweep of human history.

II

In the repudiation of chattel slavery and in the acceptance of same-sex relationships as expressions of love, there is a double movement from factual ignorance to factual knowledge and from contempt, disgust, and revulsion to sympathy and understanding. To be sure, in both instances, the movement is often interrupted and reversed. Even today it is far from complete. Yet any comparison of the starting point with the current state has to recognize the extent to which complete incomprehension has given way to glimmerings of understanding.

Cotton Mather famously argued that slave-owning is a duty. Responding to the first few doubts about the institution of slavery,[1]

---

[1] As a number of authors have shown, New World slavery began as the adaptation of forms of serfdom already present in late Medieval Europe, particularly in Portugal and

Philip Kitcher, *Problems of False Consciousness* In: *Moral Progress*. Edited by: Jan-Christoph Heilinger, Oxford University Press. © Oxford University Press 2021. DOI: 10.1093/oso/9780197549155.003.0003

he saw the predicament of the indigenous African people to be one of darkness, depravity, and savagery, with "rescue" into slavery as providing the only possible route to their eternal salvation.[2] His claims about life on the African continent were groundless, prompted by travelers' tales,[3] and refracted through a vivid theological imagination. Those who questioned the legitimacy of slavery were no better informed about conditions in Africa. Worried by different scriptural passages (Gospel injunctions to care for the poor, the downtrodden, and the stranger), they asked if the sufferings apparently inflicted on the slaves were either necessary or helpful in leading them to eternal life. Once that question had been raised, there was a prima facie case for seeing the practice of owning slaves as problematic. Moral inquiry was pursued sporadically, as outbreaks of protest were met with

Spain. By the mid-fifteenth century, sugar was being cultivated on islands off the African coast, using black African slaves. That system was later exported to the New World. For discussion of the antecedents of the practice, see David Brion Davis, *Inhuman Bondage* (New York: Oxford University Press, 2008), Chapter 4, and Robin Blackburn, *The American Crucible* (London: Verso, 2013), Chapters 1–3. Early doubts about the institution of New World slavery were voiced by Samuel Sewall in 1700 in his tract "The Selling of Joseph: A Memorial" (reprinted in Mason Lowance, ed., *Against Slavery: An Abolitionist Reader* [London: Penguin, 2000], 11–14). Sewall's biblical arguments elicited a reply from John Saffin—"A Brief Candid Answer to a Late Printed Sheet, Entitled, *The Selling of Joseph*" (Lowance, *Against Slavery*, 15–17).

[2] Cotton Mather extended Saffin's brief, arguing that "[t]he State of your *Negroes* in the World, must be low, and mean," and that, consequently, something should be "done, towards their welfare in the *World to Come*" (Lowance, *Against Slavery*, 19; see also 20). The idea of slavery as a potential means to salvation was by no means confined to the New World and to New England Puritanism. The Catholic Church of the sixteenth century approved the slave trade as a potential means of bringing infidels to Christ. See Seymour Drescher, *Abolition: A History of Slavery and Antislavery* (Cambridge: Cambridge University Press, 2009), 63.

[3] In her comments on the lectures as I delivered them in Munich, Susan Neiman rightly pointed out that the richness of indigenous African culture was recognized in the West. She asked—quite reasonably—whether Cotton Mather and his fellows were being honest in their claims about the savagery of the situation from which the New World slaves were being "rescued." The works of Davis and Blackburn (cited in note 1 earlier) are clear that the slave trade practiced by the Spanish and Portuguese was undertaken in full knowledge of African art, culture, and social organization. That earlier slave trade generated a practice of kidnapping and transporting Africans from the interior and selling them on the coast. So far as I can tell, the Yankee sea captains who ferried captive Africans across the Atlantic never went inland, and they lacked knowledge of the societies from which their victims came. Hence I'm inclined to believe that the New England Puritans were simply ignorant. Neither they, nor those who supplied them with slaves, knew what the Spanish and Portuguese had previously discovered.

reassurances about benevolent treatment (from which occasional deviations were only to be expected) and denials of the capacities of the African slaves.[4] Stereotypes of differences in "racial character" were built, disseminated, and used as a barrier against careful assessment of what the slaves could feel and what they could do. Those stereotypes halted many incipient debates, and they prevailed throughout the eighteenth century (Thomas Jefferson's hideous passage on the character of the "Negro race," in his *Notes on the State of Virginia*, is only one of the many instances of how prejudice blocked moral inquiry).[5]

Periodic protests grew out of individual encounters with fragments of the life of a slave. Some were moved to question by observing particular events—a savage beating or the anguish expressed as slaves were sold and families broken up. Others heard tales of harsh punishments and of the sexual usage of young female slaves. John Woolman's route to abolitionism, well documented in his journal, began with an incident in which he was asked to witness a contract between his master and the prospective owner of a young woman. His conscience pricked him. Uneasy at the prospect of complicity in a transfer that might cause abuse, pain, and suffering, he clutched at reassuring features of the situation: the buyer was "old" and "a Friend" (a Quaker), perhaps lessening the chances of future rape and increasing those of humane treatment.[6] Woolman's inchoate sense of wrongful—sinful—consequences blossomed in his reflections on the episode, leading him to explore. He began an unsystematic moral inquiry, seeking to learn about the conditions of life under slavery, and the capacities of the slaves. Woolman opened a conversation.

---

[4] Some defenders of slavery offer lines of argument that anticipate general defenses of inequality. The differences in treatment are taken to contribute to a state that is best for all. This form of justification is reinforced by supposing the slaves to belong to an inferior race.

[5] Thomas Jefferson, *Notes on the State of Virginia*, Query 14: Laws; the lengthy passage on racial comparison is reprinted in Merrill D. Peterson, ed., *The Portable Thomas Jefferson* (New York: Penguin, 1977), 186–193. It is hard to understand how a man who apparently enjoyed sexual relations with Sally Hemmings could have argued for an aesthetic racial hierarchy, by adverting to "the preference of the Oranootan for the black woman over those of his own species" (187), or could have supported "an effort to keep those in the department of man as distinct as nature has formed them" (193).

[6] John Woolman, *The Journal of John Woolman* (New York: Citadel Press, 1961), 14–15.

By the nineteenth century, the barriers erected by the stereotypes began to crumble.[7] Concessions were forced as serious explorations of life in Africa undermined the myth that the middle passage might constitute part of an important rescue operation. More dramatically, dialogues with slaves and ex-slaves, together with demonstrations of their abilities, refuted the standard appeals to racial inferiority. Of course, there were twists and turns. Acknowledgments of the talents displayed by Frederick Douglass were coupled with suspicions about his alleged period of enslavement. Douglass's eloquent reply is rightly famous: removing his shirt, he exposed his back to his audience, allowing them to observe the scars and stripes.[8]

Within this long process of moral change, it is possible to discern a structure with some resemblance to the process my moral maxims would recommend. Compress the history, collapse the stereotypes, focus only on the heroes, and an approximation to the ideal conversation will emerge. Around 1700, doubts are raised about the permissibility of slavery, and, a few decades later, Woolman comes to see slavery as prima facie problematic. He is moved to investigate, and he recruits followers who continue his work. Facts are uncovered, sympathy grows, and perspectives are shared. Yet abolitionism only begins to emerge as a political movement in the late eighteenth century—and, even during the Civil War, abolitionists do not constitute a majority in the Northern States. The great success of nineteenth-century abolitionism consists in allowing previously silenced voices to be heard. Slaves and ex-slaves start to contribute to the discussion. As mutual engagement grows, better-informed people begin to see slavery as a condition they cannot ask others to accept. Discussions remain at a serious remove from the requirements on ideal conversation—but they come closer.

---

[7] My formulation is deliberately cautious. Stereotypes don't magically disappear. Sometimes they evolve, shedding their early crude forms but adopting new, and more subtle, guises. Claude Steele's important studies of "stereotype threat" make plain how, despite advances since Jefferson, there is still plenty of further work to be done (see his *Whistling Vivaldi* [New York: W.W. Norton, 2010]).

[8] Note that the effect of the reply depended on previous progressive shifts, without which Douglass would not have had an audience. The history of abolitionism makes the microstructure of this revolution evident. Many smaller progressive shifts were needed.

With respect to the abolition of slavery, the voices of the oppressed were initially silenced. The public conversation began with people who were not at any obvious risk under the moral status quo.[9] Challenges to the institution of slavery started with debates among reflective Anglo-Saxon Protestants about how to read particular passages in the Bible. They were amplified by John Woolman, by some of his fellow Quakers ("Friends" is surely an apt designation for these people), and only later were the voices of the threatened and oppressed—of Sojourner Truth, Frederick Douglass, Harriet Tubman, W. E. B. DuBois, Rosa Parks, and Martin Luther King Jr.—dominant in the public debate. We should not, however, forget the unheard sufferers behind the initial challenges. Almost certainly, there are many slaves, whose names no present or future historian will ever know, whose words or whose conduct or whose demeanor played a crucial role in provoking the questions posed by those who intervened on their behalf.

To compress history in this way ignores much that actually happened, the stuttering steps forward and the lurches backward. That, of course, is the Deweyan point. Self-conscious moral inquiry would speed up the process. Instead of a century and a half, resolution of the moral challenge might have taken only a decade. Moreover, it might have been more thorough, proceeding further than has so far been managed. From the perspective of the moral maxims, the resolutions so far achieved look like awkward compromises, generated from partial efforts at perspective-sharing.[10]

The revolution in attitudes toward same-sex love has gone more speedily. Yet it's worth asking why it could not have happened earlier. Why did Stonewall spark the conversations Oscar Wilde had failed to initiate? Wilde's public persona—the insouciance and the wit—may

---

[9] Interestingly, some of the early abolitionists *take* themselves to be in danger because of the prevalent moral code. Unsatisfied with the interpretations of the scriptures cited in favor of slave-owning, they are concerned for the fate of their immortal souls, and the souls of their families and friends. Anxiety often grows, as it does with John Woolman, from a sense of personal sinfulness.

[10] They are also dominated, throughout large parts of the actual debates, by assumptions, accepted by all parties, that would be ruled out in an ideal conversation. Many of the heroes (Woolman, for example) frame their inquiries and their arguments by presupposing the moral authority of the Christian scriptures. The interpretive debates that surround uses of this strategy expose its flouting of the condition requiring the use only of justified information. For more on this point, see later discussion.

have told against him.[11] His courageous—or foolhardy?—attempt to defend "the love that dare not speak its name" ended not only in the wreck of his own life and in damage to his family but also in self-satisfied celebrations of the triumph of "proper morals" over "gross indecency."

By contrast, those who resisted the police raid on the Stonewall Inn were plainly serious, encouraging others to join in a movement of resistance. Those who fought back sparked a discussion that ended differently, because it was followed, relatively quickly, by a flood of supportive confessions. The men and women of the early 1970s who "came out," to their families, their friends, and sometimes even to their coworkers, did not need the physical courage of those who resisted the police. Nevertheless, in the prevailing moral climate, the risks they took were enormous. Of course, some of them paid a heavy price; they were ostracized by their families, deprived of long-standing friendships, and lost their jobs. The sacrifices, large or small, contributed to a cumulative expansion in the moral imagination of a startled majority. People who had railed against "perversion," who had jeered and mocked and joked, who had sometimes roughed up those they suspected, suddenly found they had acquaintances and friends, apparently "nice people," people whose kindness, generosity, loyalty, forbearance, fairness, honesty, and conscientiousness they had always respected but who turned out to have a hidden side to their lives. Moreover, as the onlookers came to understand the awful burden of keeping that side well concealed, the stereotypes began to dissolve. Images of unkempt predatory men, loitering among the scruffy bushes in deserted areas of public parks or in the vicinity of public toilets, softened into visions of anxious seekers, desperate for a moment of erotic connection, leaving with unsteady steps a world they found confining but in which they nonetheless hoped to continue to live. What could possess these friends and acquaintances, whose conduct in other moral domains appeared exemplary, to flout a taboo? As members of the broader society posed the

[11] Two decades later, Lytton Strachey emulated Wilde's strategy and got away with it. When a military tribunal reviewed his plea to be a conscientious objector, he was asked the stock question: "What would you do if you saw a German officer trying to rape your mother or your sister?" Strachey replied: "I should try to interpose my body." His refusal to serve in the armed forces was allowed.

question to themselves, they began to engage with a perspective previously dismissed as utterly alien. They came, haltingly and incompletely to be sure, to look at the world from their friends' point of view.

The actual history of these moral revolutions depends on the courage of the conversation starters and the conversation renewers, on their numbers, on their eloquence, on their persistence, and, perhaps above all, on their willingness to make large sacrifices for a cause. In the same-sex case, besides those already mentioned, we should number the same-sex couples, probably more often female than male, who quietly, patiently, and often diplomatically, reassured their neighbors that their "deviant" domestic arrangements were morally acceptable. Within a few years, a significant number of people had begun to wonder if the prevalent attitudes toward same-sex relationships were problematic. Some of those they knew were declaring—with evident courage—that enough was enough. Even lifelong homophobes began to reach into parts of the lives of their gay and lesbian friends that had previously been terra incognita.

Here, too, compression allows a loose match with my methodological model. Protest uncovers an existing situation as potentially problematic. Conversation begins not only in public fora but also—perhaps more importantly—in numerous private discussions among people who already know one another (but who now realize the limits of their mutual understanding). Social expansion of perspective-sharing and individual efforts to the same end reinforces one another. Attitudes shift, so that those who grow up in the early twenty-first century are often not only appalled but also puzzled by homophobia. Their extended sympathy finds the corresponding public expression, in the passage of laws allowing same-sex marriage, for example, entirely natural. As natural, indeed, as their grandparents would have judged such unions to be vile, sinful, and contrary to nature.

Actual history complicates the smooth line of moral inquiry, proceeding from Stonewall to *Lawrence v. Texas* and *Obergefell v. Hodges*. More-or-less ideal conversations have often been punctuated by failures of mutual engagement, most often through reliance on supposedly authoritative religious texts, but sometimes because of fears (the AIDS crisis, the potential loss of "gay culture").[12] As in

---

[12]   In the 1980s, the claim that AIDS was a divine punishment for the "sin of homosexuality" was common enough to inspire serious discussion. See Timothy F. Murphy,

the movement to overturn slavery, my methodological maxims commend a tidier process, following the contours of what has occurred but avoiding the deviations. Here, too, it meets the Deweyan demand to streamline moral progress.

A similar point holds for the historical campaign to expand women's rights. In this instance, from the very beginning, women spoke for themselves. Most of those who initiated and renewed public debates about what roles women should be allowed to play, from Mary Wollstonecraft to Catherine MacKinnon, have been from the educated classes (although, as with Sojourner Truth, there are important exceptions). In this instance, the potential roles are so numerous that many subsidiary debates proliferate. Early discussions focused on the particular contexts pertinent to the lives of women who were otherwise privileged: the right to choose their spouses, to control property, to divorce, to enter the professions, to be educated, and to qualify for university degrees. Even in the twentieth century, in the "liberation movement" of the 1960s, the concerns of white, reasonably well-off, women dominated. Greater inclusiveness has been an achievement of later feminism, involving a spread of understanding of and sympathy for female aspirations and frustrations across a wider range of social spheres. For this moral revolution, too, speech sometimes took the form of risky action. Emmeline Pankhurst went to prison for chaining herself to the railings of Buckingham Palace, and Emily Davisson's attempt to attach suffragette banners to the reins of the King's Horse, during the 1913 Derby, brought about her death.

A fully detailed treatment of this case must, however, acknowledge the important role false consciousness plays in the actual history. Whereas contact between white moralists and black slaves was often negligible, and dialogue between heterosexuals and *identifiable* homosexuals frequently limited, almost all males (including staunch champions of patriarchy) have always lived in close, amicable, even loving, relations with women (mothers, sisters, wives, daughters, and sometimes friends). We might thus expect opportunities for

"Is AIDS a Just Punishment?" *Journal of Medical Ethics* 14 (1988): 154–160. Concerns about the "normalization" of gay culture are voiced in Michael Warner, *The Trouble with Normal* (New York: The Free Press, 1999).

discussion to be readily available and for the sharing of perspectives to be easily attained. Under false consciousness, however, women do not protest their situation, and sympathetic men, committed to mutual engagement, can understandably infer the permissibility of a patriarchal status quo. Recall the loving husband and the devoted wife at the Victorian fireside. False consciousness poses a formidable obstacle to the process envisaged by my methodological maxims. Hence, a more adequate understanding of the feminist revolution can come only after the model has been further refined.

III

The approach I have adopted not only isolates and emphasizes key features of apparently progressive changes in the relatively recent past. It also makes sense of our long history as a species engaged in moral practice. As I've argued elsewhere,[13] human life has been structured by moral requirements for tens of thousands of years. I think of Plato as a footnote to the history of morality. Our collective moral project probably spans between fifty thousand and one hundred thousand years.[14]

The examples of slavery and of same-sex love point to important limitations of that project. In the actual course of the debates, stubborn refusals to identify and share in the perspectives of others are

[13] Philip Kitcher, *The Ethical Project* (Cambridge, MA: Harvard University Press, 2011).

[14] In *The Ethical Project*, I settled for the more conservative figure (fifty thousand years), taking that to be the point at which human language fully emerged. The studies of Kim Sterelny and Michael Tomasello have persuaded me that language is not a sine qua non for moral practice (see Kim Sterelny, *The Evolved Apprentice* [Cambridge, MA: MIT Press, 2012]; and Michael Tomasello, *A Natural History of Human Morality* [Cambridge, MA: Harvard University Press, 2016]). It now seems likely to me that, before the full development of language, our predecessors were already able to recognize regularities between conduct and consequences, adjusting their behavior accordingly (in his comments on *The Ethical Project* ["Morality's Dark Past," *Analyse und Kritik* 34, no. 1, 2012, 95–116], Sterelny makes a forceful case for this particular point).

Moreover, I now want to differentiate the moral project from its ethical relative. That distinction will occupy us later. For the moment, it is enough to propose the moral project as primary, and as setting the stage for the emergence of more broadly ethical issues. This is another amendment of my earlier position. Further refinements will come in subsequent discussions.

prominent. Even under the aegis of morality, failures of mutual engagement occur with depressing frequency. Those failures point to the persistence of what I shall call the *ur-problem*, the problem from which the moral project and our progress in it start.

Homo sapiens evolved as a social species of an unusual kind. Like our closest relatives, chimpanzees and bonobos, our ancestors lived in small groups, mixed by age and sex. Arrangements of this sort are fragile, vulnerable to breaking up as members of the band compete for scarce resources. Studies of our evolutionary cousins reveal the importance of cooperation, and the difficulties that ensue when internal tensions erupt. The best available picture of pre-moral hominin—and human—life portrays our predecessors as possessing a capacity for identifying the desires and intentions of their fellow band members and for adjusting their behavior so as to engage in joint projects with others.[15] More precisely, they were able to tune their behavior so as to satisfy the desires of all affected better than would have been possible without the tuning. This psychological ability, *responsiveness* to give it a name, allowed for cooperation and permitted ancestral societies to hang together.[16] Pre-moral responsiveness, in chimpanzees and

[15] The evolutionary approach I favor dovetails with important studies that have explored the preconditions for moral practice. In a series of important books, Frans De Waal has argued that the "building blocks" for morality were present in the most recent common ancestor of human beings and chimpanzees (see, in particular, his *Good Natured* [Cambridge, MA: Harvard University Press, 1997]; and *Primates and Philosophers* [Princeton, NJ: Princeton University Press, 2006]). Patricia Churchland combines philosophical analysis with evidence from neuroscience and studies of animal behavior in her characterization of the "platform" on which moral practice is built (see her *Braintrust* [Princeton, NJ: Princeton University Press, 2011]). See also Christopher Boehm, *Moral Origins* (New York: Basic Books, 2012). In my judgment, the position outlined in Russell Powell and Allen Buchanan, *The Evolution of Moral Progress* (New York: Oxford University Press, 2018) is also largely consistent with my claims, despite the efforts of the authors to portray themselves as offering an alternative view. (I'll leave it to readers of both books to decide which of these perspectives is more accurate.)

[16] In *The Ethical Project*, I took the crucial capacity to be one for psychological altruism, which I characterized in a particular way (see Chapter 1 of that book, and also my "Varieties of Altruism," *Economics and Philosophy* 26, no. 2, 2010, 121–148). My approach now seems too narrow, most obviously in its failure to include the kinds of joint projects insightfully emphasized by Stephen Darwall (*The Second Person* [Cambridge, MA: Harvard University Press, 2009]). Both Sterelny and Tomasello develop related ideas in the evolutionary context (see the works cited in note 14).

Despite this significant modification, however, many of the features of my earlier approach are preserved in my proposals in these lectures. Chapters 1–4 of *The Ethical Project* offer more extensive arguments for some of the claims made here.

among our forebears, was nevertheless incomplete. In *some* contexts, it led our predecessors to mutually beneficial behavior. But, as the observations of contemporary chimps decisively demonstrate, under many circumstances, the evolutionary adaptation to respond to others breaks down or is overridden by competing pressures.[17] The animals ignore the wishes of their erstwhile allies—or even thwart them. When that occurs, elaborate processes of peacemaking are required if group harmony is to be maintained.[18] Cooperation among chimpanzees is patchy and sporadic because the underlying psychological tendency to respond is limited. These animals have a capacity for responsiveness sufficient to enable them to live together in social groups of an unusual kind. They lack enough of that capacity to live together smoothly and easily. Group size and the extent of cooperation are bounded by the need for prolonged bouts of mutual reassurance. The animals muddle along.

So once did we. Human beings, too, share the capacity of responsiveness. Perhaps in the evolution of our species that capacity has become more extensive, so that, even without a large structure of moral and legal restraints, it would operate across a wider range of circumstances than the limited responsiveness observed among our cousins.[19] Nevertheless, as my historical examples make clear, despite the weighty pressures of a socially approved moral order, our native psychological propensities to perspective-sharing are restricted.[20] Contemporary people, all of us, readily ignore the aspirations of others, acting with indifference or even in opposition to fellow humans to whom we might bring aid or comfort.

Limited responsiveness not only underlies the fragility of chimpanzee societies. It also leads to an evolutionary cul-de-sac. A species that struggles to maintain cohesive relations among a relatively small

---

[17] Franz De Waal's *Chimpanzee Politics* (Baltimore: Johns Hopkins University Press, 1982) makes this point extremely forcefully.

[18] See Franz De Waal, *Peacemaking among Primates* (Cambridge, MA: Harvard University Press, 1990).

[19] Sarah Blaffer Hrdy's important studies of allomothering provide evidence of one important extension of responsiveness. See *Mothers and Others* (Cambridge, MA: Harvard University Press, 2011).

[20] For a psychological treatment of perspective-sharing from which I have learned much, see E. Tory Higgins, *Shared Reality* (New York: Oxford University Press, 2019).

number of animals—of the order of seventy—would find its social order stretched to the breaking point were it to attempt any substantial increase in group size. By the same token, the need to spend considerable time in breaking up and making up restricts the possibilities of fruitful cooperation. From the later Paleolithic on, our predecessors had discovered a way out of the dead end. Trade networks linking adjacent groups enabled them to use resources only found in distant places.[21] Hostility between neighbors gave way first to temporary assemblages, and eventually to the merging of different bands. Cooperation extended to allow coordinated projects of domesticating plants and animals. Almost ten thousand years before the present, human beings were living together in settlements with more than one thousand inhabitants.[22]

How were these developments possible? I offer what I take to be the obvious hypothesis. Rapid changes in the conditions of human life—and the relevant period of a few tens of thousands of years is tiny in evolutionary terms—came about not through any sudden shift in heritable psychological tendencies, but because our ancestors introduced, and quickly refined, a *social technology* for amplifying our limited pre-moral responsiveness. They invented morality. The step they took—a *progressive* change[23]—provided a partial solution to the *urproblem*: the problem of expanding human responsiveness.

---

[21] The hypothesis of trading networks in the Upper Paleolithic was originally advanced by Colin Renfrew (see C. Renfrew and S. Shennan, *Ranking, Resource, and Exchange* [Cambridge: Cambridge University Press, 1982]). This work was based on discovery of obsidian tools at a significant distance from the nearest source of obsidian. There is now extensive archeological evidence for trading routes at least 15,000 years ago. Some archeologists have argued that African trade developed significantly earlier; see S. McBrearty and A. S. Brooks, "The Revolution That Wasn't," *Journal of Human Evolution* 39 (2000): 453–563.

[22] The most famous of these are Jericho and Çatal Hüyük. There has been significant debate on whether these settlements should be called "cities" or simply seen as "overgrown villages." According to Ian Hodder, the principal authority on Çatal Hüyük, that question is best abandoned in favor of inquiry into how such settlements functioned. The evidence currently available suggests little differentiation among houses (and thus a relatively egalitarian society) and limited agriculture (see, for example, Ian Hodder, "Çatal Hüyük: The Leopard Changes Its Spots. A Summary of Recent Work," *Anatolian Studies* 64 [2014]: 1–22, especially 5).

[23] Should it be counted as *morally* progressive? I'm inclined to think of it as *socially* progressive (in roughly the sense suggested in my "Social Progress") and as introducing the conditions under which moral progress can occur. It creates the conditions under which it can retrospectively be viewed as a moral advance. But there is something

Almost certainly, the first ventures were crude. The pioneers focused on the most salient examples of socially disruptive behavior,
failure to share with others, the initiation of violence, and the like.
Patterns of expected conduct were instituted, with conformity to
them encouraged by threats of painful punishments for deviation. Of
course, even if these legislative efforts were facilitated through the at-
tainment of full human language, the inventors could not have framed
their achievements in the terms I have used. They responded to the
observed *symptoms* of a problematic underlying condition. Like most
of the healers in human history, they worked without explicit understanding of the causal factors at work.

Once the moral project was under way, it was probably developed
in ways akin to those practiced among the few surviving hunter-
gatherers. Problems encountered by group members are raised and
discussed "in the long cool hour."[24] Adults exchange their perceptions
of what has occurred and aim to arrive at resolutions with which all
of them can live. Surely they do not always appeal to the best available information, nor are they completely mutually engaged, and
younger band members are typically absent (represented only by
their older relatives). Nonetheless these conversations are recogniz-
able as approximations of the kind of deliberation I have viewed as
central to moral methodology. Indeed, they may well approximate
the requirements of moral method more closely than virtually all the
attempts at moral inquiry pursued during the past ten thousand years.

For moral practice has changed enormously during its long career. Some of those changes are surely welcome, rightly recognized
in retrospect as progressive. As I have already remarked, the efforts
of the pioneers were crude reactions to the troublesome symptoms
they perceived. Not only has the array of rules, moral exemplars, and

worryingly self-fulfilling about hailing the invention of the moral project as a moral advance. Perhaps it is best to think of the transition simply as a progressive step (no further
characterization) in human history.

[24] I am grateful to Amia Srinivasan, whose sensitive review of *The Ethical Project*
(*London Review of Books* 34, no. 23 [2012]: 17–18) used this phrase as its title. Her focus
on my proposed method of moral inquiry has helped me to see how to improve my presentation of my approach, and it has thus inspired the project of these lectures.

patterns of conduct grown in extent during subsequent millennia, but the psychological processes behind people's conformity to them have also become far more complex. External punishment gives way to internal sanctions, not through any heritable biological change, but through a social accomplishment. Successful societies have learned how to bring up proper moral agents, educating them to instill solidarity within the group, pride in the ways in which "we do things," admiration for those who act most spectacularly on behalf of the common good, and respect for the "moral law" that enhances group and individual welfare. Cultural evolution—far more rapid than its biological counterpart—has worked this magic, creating complex moral practices that have changed human life.

And it has changed human beings as well. Not only do we live in vastly larger societies, bound together by unsurveyable networks of causal connections, not only are our lives shaped by division of labor, multiple roles and interlocking institutions, but the *conceptions* we can have and the *emotions* we can feel are themselves made possible by the moral project. Morality, as I understand it, focuses primarily on our interactions with others, and derivatively on how we should develop ourselves to prepare for those interactions.[25] With the advent of differentiated roles arises a new question: How to live? Ethical life, concerned not only with what should be done but also with the question of what kind of person someone should aspire to be, is generated from the moral project, once moral practice has assumed sufficient complexity.[26]

---

[25] I take self-regarding duties to center initially on the capacities needed for morally required actions within the social group. With the emergence of ethical life (as characterized later), those duties obtain a further grounding through their role in how a person should be.

[26] Thus the "ancient"—and central—philosophical question of the good life emerges from a long prior history of moral practice. My distinction between the moral and the ethical follows Bernard Williams (*Ethics and the Limits of Philosophy* [Cambridge, MA: Harvard University Press, 1986]), although it differs from his account in its historical compass. Answers to questions about living well seem to me to be clearly context relative. The general form of the best contemporary approaches include the following: John Rawls, *A Theory of Justice* (Cambridge, MA: Harvard University, Press, 1971), §§ 63–67; Bernard Williams, "Persons, Character, and Morality," in *Moral Luck* (Cambridge: Cambridge University Press, 1981); and Susan Wolf, *Meaning in Life and Why It Matters* (Princeton, NJ: Princeton University, 2010). These seem to me entirely unsuited to such questions as they might be posed for our distant ancestors, and, very

Many of the specific changes featuring in the long evolutionary process I have so sketchily reviewed should count as exemplars of moral progress. One striking example is the shift from the original form of the lex talionis to the familiar version: at some time between three and four thousand years ago, people decided against punishing a man who had murdered someone else's daughter by killing the culprit's daughter. Yet, besides the welcome modifications, marked by the features my maxims bring into prominence, there have also been moral losses. One I want to highlight concerns the falling away from moral methodology. To repeat, many of the investigations of the early stages of the moral project were closer approximations to the advice of my moral maxims than the inquiries of more recent millennia.

Democratic contractualism has lapsed. Instead, our moral thinking is dominated by the conception of individual moral authorities. Most commonly, those authorities are deities, or their mundane representatives—the shamans, the seers, the chosen teachers, and the priests. Not everyone sees such people as the appropriate sources of moral enlightenment. One tribe, to which I belong, the philosophers, often suppose moral discoveries to be available to those who can undergo particular kinds of processes, following reason, or sentiment, or intuition. Of course, the allegedly authoritative deliverances are often preceded by discussions involving several people, but they tend to include those whose views and whose criteria for amending their views fall within a very narrow range. Religious leaders consult privileged members of the flock; philosophers try out their ideas on their colleagues (frequently on the like-minded—the few "competent judges"—members of a tiny elite). Contemporary versions of the gathering of the whole band in the long, cool hour are rare.[27]

likely, for most of the human beings who have ever lived (including some who live today).

[27] One context in which serious exchange among people with different viewpoints occurs is when institutional review boards scrutinize proposals for research involving experiments on animals. Even here, however, the composition is skewed toward a particular group (biomedical scientists). As I have argued (in "Experimental Animals," *Philosophy and Public Affairs* 43, no. 4 [2015]: 287–311), a greater representation of people afflicted by diseases for which the research might promise relief would improve

What explains the departure from democratic contractualism? There's a benign answer. The moral project facilitated, more than twenty thousand years ago, an expansion of the network of causal interactions among human beings, culminating in the complex web of contemporary human life. Today, it would be impossible to emulate the inclusive deliberations of those pioneering Paleolithic bands. Human societies have had to divide the labor, assigning to those best qualified the job of pronouncing on moral matters. Yet, if my proposals about the proper character of moral inquiry are correct, this is not so much an adaptation of proper procedures to a context in which their exact implementation is no longer feasible as a desertion of moral methodology by substituting something completely different. Why are there so few attempts to *approximate* an inclusive, fully informed, mutually engaged discussion? Why, in short, have more recent versions of the moral project settled for a strategy *that builds in exclusion from the start*? If, as I have suggested, the ur-problem concerns a limitation we all share—our limited capacity for responding to others—it would seem to be an error to suppose that a few individuals should have the last word.

Beguiled by the moral Discovery View, all the major traditions of moral practice have taken insight to be something individual people could achieve if they were blessed or particularly talented or able to think with special clarity and rigor. The bewitchment is not accidental. From the beginnings of the moral project, all human groups, small and large alike, have faced the problem of fostering compliance to the agreed-upon patterns of conduct. If actions were always open to public scrutiny, the difficulty would be greatly lessened, perhaps disappearing entirely. Even in the most tightly-knit communities, however, people slip away from view. How are the foragers and hunters to be kept in line, when, in efforts to increase the resources the group needs, they go their separate ways? The anthropological record offers an answer, apparently universally adopted. Nobody is ever entirely out of sight. For there is always a being (or beings, or forces) who surveys (or reacts to) what is done, and deviations from proper behavior will call down

the deliberation—as would the inclusion of knowledgeable guardians of the animals on whom the experiments would be done.

terrible consequences for the malefactor (and possibly for others as well).[28]

The story presupposes harmony between the moral code prevailing within the group and the predilections of the hidden being. The watcher in the sky must agree with the resolutions achieved in the long cool hour and must be moved to anger when they are violated. Already there's the germ of a subversive possibility. Democratic discussion would become redundant if a more direct route to the watcher's tastes could be discovered. Claims to have found that access are decisive moments in the distortion of the moral project. When individual people, perhaps quite sincerely, or perhaps out of a wish to exert influence, convinced their fellows of their powers to discern the deity's preferences, the authority tacitly attributed to a hidden being was transferred to a local representative. The group's resolutions accord with those the deity would command, and the shaman—the seer, the priest—can enter states in which the character of the deity's inclinations becomes transparent. Perhaps the new role is initially modest. The putative understanding of the divine mind gives the privileged observer greater weight in the moral deliberations. The long career of the priesthood, evident in the remnants of sacrifices, ceremonies, totems, and sacred figures, suggests, however, that, as societies grew larger, the difficulties of bringing the group together for inevitably lengthy deliberations gave way to a simpler solution. Let those whom the gods have chosen perform their rites and consult their oracles—and then tell everyone what should be done.

Contemporary morality is heir to that repudiation of democratic contractualism, and not merely when people claim (as is still often the case) a religious foundation for morality. For over two millennia, secular philosophy has worried about the claim. In the *Euthyphro*, Plato posed an important dilemma for it. Kant deepened the point by

---

[28] See Edward Westermarck, *The Origin and Development of the Moral Ideas* (London: Macmillan & Co., 1926), volume 2, Chapter 50, "Gods as Guardians of Morality." I don't suggest that unseen observers ("transcendent policemen") were originally hypothesized to solve the compliance problem. More likely, our predecessors appealed to hidden persons or hidden impersonal forces to explain aspects of nature beyond their abilities to control, and they later extended the view to include ideas of surveillance and punishment, thus increasing the chances of lone individuals' complying with the moral code.

noting how a responsible decision to obey a command depends not only on recognizing the commander's power but also his moral qualities (or the moral qualities of the command itself). Religious texts and traditions can only provide moral guidance if human beings possess some independent means for appreciating the goodness of their sources. Yet the secular shift merely transmutes the individualism of the (far more popular) religious conception of morality. Shamans and priests are discredited. But authority passes to other privileged people (moral philosophers or professional ethicists), those who can discern the structure of the moral law or who can engage in special processes of moral reflection.

I have no doubt that there are differences in human capacities for moral decision. Nor do I underestimate the role moral philosophy can play in helping collective deliberation to come closer to the democratic ideal. The distortion I have tried to trace in the career of the moral project lies in replacing the idea of justified moral resolution as resulting from a particular type of conversation with that of individual discovery; discovery occurs either through access to some unimpeachable authority or through the fathoming of something fixed prior to and independent of human efforts to work through problems together.

The effects of that distortion are vividly present in the historical examples of progress, specifically in the moments of reversal. Those who angrily rejected the appeals of early abolitionists often based their refusals to listen on their "knowledge" of where moral authority lay. Wilde's accusers summoned their own body of "supportive evidence." For two centuries, critics of "radical feminism" have used their observations to denounce a movement of bitter, frustrated, negligent, irresponsible, unhappy half-women: "bluestocking" has been a relatively mild epithet. Champions of the individualist picture will reply, of course, by offering a different diagnosis. The misguided people who resisted progressive steps looked in the wrong places. They consulted the wrong texts, or they misinterpreted what they read, or they relied on a scattered set of unrepresentative observations, or they failed to engage in the appropriate thought experiments, or their reasoning failed to universalize in the proper way, or . . . The difficulty, I suggest, is deeper. To proceed as individualists recommend is to invite exclusion. Exclusion, we might say, has become the name of the moral game.[29]

IV

The stage is now set for considering false consciousness. Although it is entangled with moral deafness in all three of my examples, the intertwining is particularly prominent in the protracted debates about women's proper role. The women who clamor for the chance to do things currently forbidden to them are dismissed as unwomanly, defective, embittered, even monstrous.

Defenders of the status quo place great weight on the fact that "most women" or "normal women" do not complain but enjoy the roles tradition has assigned them. Most of the wounded do not even cry. Thus it is easy to marginalize the few who do. Again and again, the proposed expansion of opportunities is castigated as harmful on the grounds that it will undermine the happiness of women, forcing them to take on burdens that the majority—the "healthy" women—do not wish to carry. Because those who protest alleged restrictions are deviant, their perspectives are improperly formed. It would be as wrong to attempt to sympathize with their points of view as it would with the "perspective" of a thoroughly antisocial criminal. What appears as moral deafness is seen as a justified refusal to extend sympathy in the wrong directions. Moreover, justification gains strength from the many women who can be enlisted as allies in rejecting the call to engage with the "feminist perspective." Nor, historically, are those women always conscripts, summoned by men as sincere supportive witnesses. Some of them volunteer.

In this moral revolution, and, to a lesser extent, in both the others, the existence of false consciousness provides camouflage for exclusion.

[29] These conclusions don't release people from individual attempts to make moral decisions. It would be absurd to suppose that, whenever any of us faces a moral problem requiring deliberation, some group has to be assembled for purposes of discussion! The point is that our individual deliberations should try to follow the contours of the conversation the pertinent group would have. For further elaboration of this point, see the discussion of individual moral practice in the following chapter.

Consequently, the methodology provided in previous sections has a more limited scope than my formulations may well have led you to suppose. Whenever those who oppose change could use the false consciousness of some members of the oppressed group to justify their refusal to engage with the perspectives of the plaintiffs, conversations arranged in accordance with the conditions I have proposed will not deliver reform. Nor should anyone assume that the traditionalists are guilty of duplicity, as if they said to themselves (or to one another): "Aha! We can use the opinions of right-thinking women to discredit the others." Many of them were sincere and well-intentioned, earnestly committed to making women's lives go as well as possible.

Retrospectively, it's not hard to diagnose what has happened to the women whose "proper" attitudes are celebrated by champions of the status quo. Profoundly immersed in the conventional wisdom of their societies, they have come to adopt exactly the vision of themselves prescribed by tradition. Other options for living lie beyond their horizons, and they react with incomprehension, even with horror, when some of their contemporaries seek to pursue forbidden alternatives. Without their ever having made a reflective choice, the perspective designed for them by others seems uniquely correct.

After the revolution, their reaction will appear as expressing a limitation on their lives. They have been confined by the society in which they have been bred. They have not been free to become the people they might have been. Even if they would have elected to pursue exactly the activities approved for them by tradition, their lives have been diminished by the absence of a choice.

At this point in the discussion, proper understanding of the status of moral practice requires recognizing the relation between the moral and the ethical. As I use the terms, morality focuses on questions about how people should act, while ethics considers what kind of person one should be.[30] Ethics is the more inclusive sphere. That is because the standards for living well include—but are not exhausted by—the

---

[30] This seems in accord with the usages of others who do not treat "moral" and "ethical" as synonyms. Since the influential writings of Bernard Williams (particularly *Ethics and the Limits of Philosophy*), many philosophers have drawn the distinction as I have done.

standards for acting well. Yet I suggest that the moral project is historically primary. Our ancestors began that project by considering how people—originally members of the same small band—should act toward one another (in a limited range of situations). Imperatives concerning individual self-development—prescribing self-regarding duties—came later. Some of them may initially have stemmed from indirect impacts on the lives of others. To be able to perform as morally required in certain kinds of interactions may depend on acquiring particular skills, so that obligations regarding conduct toward others generate obligations of self-development. Once ethical questions have emerged, once the ethical project generalizes the moral project, commitments to living in a particular way reinforce some self-regarding duties and also entail new ones.

Here I diverge from Bernard Williams's approach to the relation between morality and ethics, for Williams views the ethical questions as primary.[31] Surveying the trajectories of ethics and morality from the ancient world to the present, he views moral questions as derived from ethical questions in ancient Greek thought, and he takes the detachment of moral inquiry from ethical inquiry to be an unfortunate deviation. (It would have been better, in his view, always to approach the question "What to do?" in light of the question "How to be?") My departure from Williams is doubly motivated. First, where he is concerned with moral and ethical *theory*, I am interested in moral and ethical *practice*. Second, even if theorizing about ethics and morality starts in the ancient world, with the Greeks, moral and ethical practice have a vastly longer history. On my evolutionary account, where the role of natural selection becomes outweighed by that of cultural selection, the origins of the project lie in simple moral questions where human limited responsiveness first makes itself felt. The social tensions symptomatic of the underlying disease (the limitations of our capacity for responding to others) manifest themselves in episodes where band members refuse to share important resources or when they initiate aggression toward some of their fellows. Straightforward injunctions to share and to refrain from attacking other band members

---

[31] Bernard Williams, *Ethics and the Limits of Philosophy* and also *Shame and Necessity* (Berkeley: University of California Press, 2008).

are the beginnings of what will flower into ethical life as we know it. Our ancestors began with *moral* prescriptions. The moral project comes first.

In the earliest stages of the moral project, ethical questions make no sense. Portraying hunter-gatherers, struggling to assemble what is needed to keep the band going and focused on what will occur in the immediate future, as asking "What kind of person should I be?" or "How do I live a meaningful life?" is the stuff of cartoons. When that ethical question arises, and is taken seriously, as it is in some parts of ancient Greece, we should note the social background against which it emerges. The question is posed, and discussed, by members of a small privileged group, free high-born men. Slaves, menial laborers, and the women (confined to their quarters) might well never have considered alternatives to what was socially prescribed for them.[32]

Nevertheless, the Greek version of the ethical question—How to live?—doesn't erupt out of nowhere. It was prepared by developments in human social life, themselves made possible by the evolution of the moral project. In societies governed by explicitly formulated rules of conduct and by approved patterns of behavior, it becomes possible to assign different roles to participants in joint enterprises. Between the origin of the moral project and the formation of the first cities, our ancestors invented the division of labor. With a differentiation of roles comes the possibility of occupying one rather than another, and thus a potential choice of how to direct activities within the social enterprise. "What kind of person should I be?" takes on a minimal sense.

More importantly, the moral project brought forth new possibilities of human relationships. The stability achieved by agreed-upon rules for behavior allows particular people to coordinate in joint activity.

---

[32] What is crucial here is the ability to *recognize* other options, even if there is no chance of realizing them. Many people who live today, and probably a significant number of our predecessors, have been able to envisage alternative possibilities for their own lives, even to yearn for the kinds of lives enjoyed by others, while understanding the conditions preventing them from living like that. Human beings can be confined by boundaries that debar them from ways of being they can identify, forms of life they regretfully, even bitterly, understand as unavailable to people like them. In emphasizing the fact that certain types of ethical questions may sometimes be irrelevant, I am concerned with the *conceptual* boundaries to human self-interpretation. I am grateful to Rahel Jaeggi and Isabel Kaeslin for helping me to see that my original formulation needed to be qualified.

Cooperating with the same partner on repeated occasions may lead to shared joy in the successes achieved—and eventually the positive feelings arise out of the coordination itself.[33] Our ancestors became able to see working with particular people as a source of satisfaction. Against the background of that capacity, older impulses were accompanied by new forms of appreciation and recognition. Our ancestors came to feel emotions beyond the repertoire of their predecessors. The "friendships" witnessed in chimpanzees that associate together, sometimes for the better part of a lifetime, took on new dimensions.[34] They became the real thing.

Once human social life had introduced a variety of roles, and once individual people recognized the possibilities of various kinds of relationships with those around them, there were genuinely alternative ways of living. Quite different lives could exemplify the morally approved patterns of conduct. In the first cities of the ancient world, and even in the pastoral societies that preceded them, some people probably had the opportunity to pose an ethical question and to try to answer it.

Even before the attempts of the Greeks to delineate goals for "the good life," the practices of our ancestors probably embodied an implicit differentiation of the qualities of lives. Richard Lee's illuminating studies of the lives of Kalahari hunter-gatherers reveal how the egalitarianism they prize has to be carefully maintained.[35] Quite possibly, their tacit recognition of some kinds of lives as particularly valuable—as models for the young—was sometimes expressed in explicit judgment. Tales of heroes are likely to have played an important role in inspiring the development of children for tens of thousands of years, issuing eventually in the oldest literary works to have survived.

Two features of the emergence of ethical reflection deserve emphasis. First, the question "How to live?" presupposes a social self. From what we can discern from the lives of contemporary hunter-gatherers,

---

[33] See my The Ethical Project, §21.

[34] See Jane Goodall, The Chimpanzees of Gombe (Cambridge, MA: Harvard University Press, 1986).

[35] The procedure for attributing the deaths of prey animals to a particular member of the hunting band is a striking example of this. See Richard Lee, The!Kung San (Cambridge: Cambridge University Press, 1979), 246–247.

it seems likely that the formative tales of our preliterate ancestors were similar to the ancient myths and sagas in embedding the hero within a community. To live well is to achieve great things for that community, to sustain it in times of severe difficulty or to transform its conditions of existence for the better. The idea of an individual living well by pursuing a freely chosen project, a project with no necessary connection to the lives of others, is an abstraction—and a distortion of the central question of ethical life. Modern approaches to ethical issues often sever the intimate connection between asking "How to live?" and "How to live *together*?"[36]

Second, formulations of these questions are often promiscuous in using adjectives. Should the followers of Socrates focus on the *happy* life, or the *good* life, or the *fully human* life, or the *meaningful* life (and there are other possibilities)? Sometimes discussions treat the phrases as equivalent, offering relief from stylistic monotony. Yet the overtones are plainly different, and it is easy to imagine people, living under very different circumstances, viewing one of the characterizations as primary, and even failing to understand the point of others. For most of our history as a species, to the extent that ethical questions arose, they would seem to concern happiness—and the avoidance of misery.[37]

From this perspective, the classical discussions of the ancient world can be understood as reactions to a previously dominant hedonism. Yet, whether or not particular ancient writers mischaracterized the views they opposed, contemporary discussions clearly distort the debate by adopting the individualist abstraction. I conjecture that the ethical life of tens of thousands of years, for most of the period during which human beings have asked "How to live?," has had no interest in orgasmatrons[38] or similar devices for private pleasure. Hedonism

[36] Mill's individualistic formulation has influenced the best subsequent discussions of the good (or "meaningful") life. See, for example, those of John Rawls, Susan Wolf, and Bernard Williams. Dewey's group-level presentation at the beginning of *The Public and Its Problems* (*Later Works*, Volume 2) provides an important corrective.

[37] My Benthamite formulation reflects Mill's melancholy judgment at the end of *A System of Logic* (Volume 8 of the *Collected Works* [Toronto: University of Toronto Press, 1974], 952) to the effect that considerations of pleasure and absence of pain reflect the dominant concerns of the majority of people who have ever lived, people who have been mired in "the puerile condition" of humanity.

[38] Woody Allen, dir., *Sleeper* (1973); the way was already paved in Aldous Huxley's *Brave New World* (1932).

starts as *communal* hedonism. Communal hedonists intend to relieve pain and spread joy among their neighbors. As they prepare for the harvest festival or the dances to celebrate the spring, they may well have found the best answer, given their circumstances, to the Socratic question. If at a later stage, *some* fortunate people have the opportunity to strive for more, to aim for the "meaningful life" even with some sacrifice of happiness, it is well to remember that the vast majority of those living now do not. Their professions of hedonism should be understood, rather than dismissed with a sneer. Especially when their claim, "Life's about having a bit of fun," doesn't stop there, but adds "with me mates."

The evolution of ethical life within a community generates *ideals of the self*. These ideals embody the features recognized by that community as figuring in a life worth aiming at. When members of the community appreciate those ideals, they are equipped with some understanding of how to make their lives go better than they otherwise would. To the extent that they can realize some of the crucial features or make up for the lack of those features, they may acquire a deeper sense of satisfaction with how they have spent their time. As they age, they not only relish the happy moments but regard the pattern of their lives as well chosen. Because human lives are inextricably linked to other lives, satisfaction must derive from a recognition of positive contributions to members of a broader community, a community that will survive after they no longer exist. Fundamental to living well is adding to something larger than the individual self, something that endures across generations, a human project.[39]

Ideals of the self serve communities well when they enable the members of those communities to make the contributions that justifiably bring this form of reflective satisfaction. Yet there are two major ways in which ideals of the self may fail to serve this function. In each case, the situation is morally problematic. The more obvious scenario occurs when the ideals available to people demand far more resources than those people have at their disposal. However they choose, the individuals in question are doomed to be dissatisfied with the course of

---

[39]   In a passage of (atypical) eloquence, Dewey's *A Common Faith* closes by celebrating this theme (*Later Works*, Volume 9).

their lives. The less obvious possibility arises when the society restricts the class of people who might adopt particular ideals.[40]

False consciousness is a consequence of the latter case. Although Mill's detachment of individual choice from the framing context of the socially embedded self distorts the discussion of how to live, his celebration of the importance of autonomy is profoundly insightful. Recognizing that the sense of having chosen one's own path enhances the satisfaction of successfully pursuing it is a progressive step in the evolution of ethical life. Once autonomous choice of the life project is included as a necessary part of any ideal of the self, those who feel that the pattern of their lives has been thrust upon them are justified in being dissatisfied. Mill's mistake lay in treating autonomy as a condition of living well for abstracted individuals, existing in some fictitious context of social isolation. He thereby created a pseudo-problem with which his successors have valiantly wrestled: how to circumscribe the "life plans" or "projects" that can be chosen autonomously, so as to exclude those that appear utterly worthless?[41] If the self had been conceived, from the beginning, as enmeshed in social relations, the idea of a "suitable life project" as consisting in promoting the lives of others would have appeared obvious.

Because we are social beings, shaped from the first by immersion in a tradition, our autonomous choice is inevitably a matter of degree. The possibilities open to us are those the community allows: indeed those it allows to *people like us*. False consciousness is the product of situations in which the community's moral practice declares that some ideals of the self are appropriate for one group within the community but not for the rest, when some members of the latter group could *in principle* profitably pursue the ideals denied to them, and when at least some members of that group acquiesce in the moral

---

[40] This can occur in two distinct ways: a community may introduce moral or legal sanctions aimed at deterring members of a particular group from living according to an ideal of the self available to others; or some people who aspire to a particular ideal may lack the resources to pursue it successfully. My concept of false consciousness focuses on the first possibility. (But some instances of the second should also provoke moral concern—see the final section of the following chapter.)

[41] The standard example is that of the person who aims to count the blades of grass in a particular area. See John Rawls, *A Theory of Justice* (Cambridge, MA: Harvard University Press, 1971), 432.

claim that those ideals are not for them. The extreme case of false consciousness occurs when all members of the community agree with this aspect of the moral practice. When false consciousness prevails to this extent, there will be no complaints about the restriction of the ideals. Hence, any discussion of the kind I envisaged in coping with exclusion will preserve the status quo. More common, however, will be situations in which, while a few members of the group for whom the ideals are viewed as inappropriate protest, many others acquiesce in their assigned roles. As I noted earlier, when that happens, advocates of tradition can appeal to widespread acceptance (by "normal" members of the group) to undermine the perspectives of those who clamor for change.

Freedom in choosing one's life plan is important. Yet this type of freedom is a matter of degree, and the options available to people have large effects on how they live. The restriction is potentially problematic, precisely because removing an obstacle to greater freedom would count as moral progress. Hence arises a spur to moral inquiry, to investigating the status of the current restrictions as justified.

On this basis, I propose an addition to the methodological maxims presented earlier.

10. Even in the absence of challenges, societies should periodically assess whether restrictions on the appropriateness of ideals of the self for some subgroups can be justified. As in other cases of moral inquiry, urgency is measured through attempts to estimate the suffering and confinement caused if the orthodox assumptions about appropriateness of ideals turned out to be unwarranted.

Periodic review is needed to handle the extreme instances of false consciousness.

The more common cases—in which a few protest—can be addressed if deliberations about justification for the complaint are preceded by investigating whether extending the scope of the ideal might provide an increase in the chances of pursuing projects that would bring reflective satisfaction. Hence, I add another maxim to treat the cases in which exclusion is entangled with false consciousness.

11. Any moral inquiry in which claims about the proper restrictions on ideals of the self are employed to support the view that the perspectives of the challengers should not be targets of sympathetic engagement should generate a secondary inquiry into the aptness of those ideals for people who are currently viewed as unsuited to adopting them.

But how exactly are inquiries about the proper scope of ideals of the self to be conducted?

Through experimentation: John Stuart Mill and Harriet Taylor countered mid-Victorian arguments by pointing out how their opponents begged the question.[42] Those who denied opportunities to take on particular roles claimed to know that women were unsuited to pursue the goals to which they aspired. They also rejected proposals to test that alleged piece of knowledge, on the grounds that such trials would cause great suffering and unhappiness. Justifying a refusal to test in this way presupposes the correctness of the view under discussion. A disputed question is settled by dogmatic assertion.

By contrast, those (like Mill and Taylor) who favored allowing the experiment to go forward were by no means committed to assuming that the outcomes would be happy ones. To celebrate the importance of autonomy in choosing the pattern of one's life does not exclude the possibility of freely choosing a path that culminates in great unhappiness. Those who volunteer as social guinea pigs, hoping that their favored "experiments of living" will open up new possibilities for themselves and for others, may be counseled, or urged to reflect, but they should not be prevented from taking risks and exposing themselves to potential suffering. Ethically defensible trials should involve people who can sincerely declare, "I have thought about the possibly disastrous consequences, and, if my aspirations are misguided, I would prefer to make my own mistakes." If there are chances of indirect impacts on others, on people who have not consented to participate, the trial should be set up in ways that shield them from harm. Social

---

[42] See John Stuart Mill and Harriet Taylor, *On the Subjection of Women*, in *The Collected Works of John Stuart Mill*, Volume 21 (Toronto: University of Toronto Press, 1984).

experiments may be painful, but if the pain is borne solely by people who have clamored to take part in them, they should be recognized for what they are: ways of moving beyond a dogmatic defense of ortho-doxy and making ethical progress by revising ideals of the self.[43]

The principal difficulty with my recommendation to make progress through experimentation is not whether trials should begin but rather when they should end. The history of social experiments and of sub-sequent reactions to them offers vivid reminders of how the outcomes are disputed. A variety of movements, from the Levellers of the seven-teenth century through the Owenites of the early nineteenth century to the enthusiasts for Israeli kibbutzim, have hoped to demonstrate the possibility of functioning communities living on terms of equality. They can point to positive features of the special arrangements they devised. Skeptics counter by emphasizing the failures, in particular the fact that none of the social groups in any of these instances endured. Can anyone reasonably expect that issues about the appropriateness of ideals of the self can be settled by trying to institute the proposed conditions and obtaining a decisive indicator of success or failure?

These worries can be addressed in two ways. First, it is salutary to reflect on the career of experimentation in the natural sciences. On numerous occasions, a test has been set up in a straightforward way, and taken to deliver a particular verdict, only for that verdict to be reversed after a more intricate experimental setup has been devised. The need for skill in *making* experiments work is—rightly—a cliché of contemporary science studies.[44] (That point is easily appreciated by people like me, complete klutzes in the lab; my adolescent efforts were

---

[43] The moral standards for social experiments are, I suggest, to be modeled on those for medical testing of new modes of treatment. Many of the interventions that now pro-long and transform human lives have been products of series of trials whose potential for harm was clearly recognized in advance. In Chapter 3 of her powerful memoir, *The Scar* (New York: W.W. Norton, 2019), Mary Cregan reviews the history of using electro-convulsive therapy to treat depression. To the extent that patients were misled or were coerced into participating, the experiments are morally problematic. However, when those who volunteered were fully aware of the risks, and who knew that no other avail-able treatment would help them, the decision to provide them with the *possibility* of relief seems entirely justified. I am urging a parallel attitude toward social experimentation.

[44] See, for example, Harry Collins, *Changing Order* (Chicago: University of Chicago Press, 1992). Collins combines insightful accounts of experimental practice with ten-dentious conclusions about the inconclusiveness of scientific debates.

not hailed as brilliant refutations of the laws of physics; my teachers simply told me to try again.) With respect to social experiments, the possibilities of refining the conditions of previous tests are vastly expanded. Hence, it is quite possible for trials to undergo an extensive sequence of adjustments before some stable pattern finally emerges. We can expect ventures in social experimentation to exemplify, on a larger scale, the features observed in the history of the natural sciences. The fact that experimental efforts to settle an important question may be inconclusive over a long period does not entail that experimental resolution is impossible.[45]

I have tacitly adopted a criterion for when social experiments end: those devising the experiments recognize conditions for setting up the trial that regularly produce a particular outcome. With respect to expansion of ideals of the self and the uncovering of false consciousness, a positive conclusion would consist in identifying ways of adjusting social arrangements so as to produce situations in which members of the group previously excluded from the ideal live satisfying lives in pursuing it; nor does their pursuit cause suffering or dissatisfaction at a comparable scale to other people in their society. The difficulties noted by the defenders of orthodoxy in their critique of earlier versions of the experiments diminish to the point at which they are judged to be small costs in relation to the large human benefits.

This criterion enables my second line of response to the worries about the inevitable indecisiveness of experiments. For history does sometimes show how a stable pattern emerges and how the criterion is met. The Victorians with whom Mill and Taylor debated prophesied all kinds of doom if women were allowed various opportunities: to manage property, to attend universities, to vote, to work full time even after marriage, to become doctors, lawyers, or to serve in the armed forces, and so forth. The orthodox feared that reforms would result in unhappiness for the women, as well as damage to domestic and family life, neglect of children, disruptions of community, and other negative effects. There have surely been social experiments—clumsy trials, as we might retrospectively see them—producing some of these

---

[45] See the illuminating discussion in Peter Galison, *How Experiments End* (Chicago: University of Chicago Press, 1987).

predicted consequences. Yet later versions of the test have learned from the unfortunate outcomes, taking steps to protect against the particular negative effects. Even today, it would be silly to declare that the experiment has been perfected. (The revolution, we might say, isn't yet complete.) Nonetheless, the overwhelming increase in quality of life for women who have seized the opportunities once denied them dwarfs the difficulties we continue to attempt to minimize. Those who reiterate the gloomy critiques of the past (and who sometimes yearn for a world in which women "know their proper place") fail to satisfy the condition of mutual engagement. The perspectives of the many women who have benefited from expanded opportunities are completely alien to them.

I'll close by considering an obvious worry. The situations in which false consciousness is present are those in which an ideal of the self is already appreciated in a society, but taken to be appropriate for only some of its members. Isn't there a deeper form of false consciousness in which an ideal of the self apt for all of us is simply not recognized? So, for example, there have been many communities throughout history in which all roles have been assigned without any choice on the part of those who occupy them. Sons and daughters who belong to particular castes must live in a specific way whether they like it or not. Thus, it might be urged, the society-wide failure to appreciate the importance of autonomy in living well is a more fundamental type of false consciousness than the kinds of predicaments that motivate my characterization.

I accept the charge. My concept of false consciousness is restricted, and it could be expanded in the suggested way. From the point of advancing moral progress, however—aiming to make it more sure-footed than it has been—extending the concept is beside the point. How might one offer methodological maxims for introducing ideals of the self that nobody has yet formulated, that lie far beyond the conceptual horizons of the community?[46] A bland recommendation to think imaginatively about possibilities of living well is surely even less

---

[46] In her penetrating book, *Critique of Forms of Life* (Cambridge, MA: Harvard University Press, 2019), Rahel Jaeggi aims to characterize a form of social critique that will (in a certain sense) be both latent in the form of life of a society and outside its conceptual horizons. If her attempt to develop the critical theory of the Frankfurt School succeeds, it would yield a broader notion of false consciousness and, perhaps, a more ambitious way of coming to terms with the predicament I envisage here. There

helpful than my admittedly vague maxims. Perhaps an analogy will help. A truly ambitious methodologist might hope to devise ways of propelling a community of natural philosophers from Aristotelian physics to relativity theory and quantum theory without a detour through classical dynamics. That venture strikes me as hopelessly utopian. In restricting the notion of false consciousness, I am trying to streamline the kinds of moral progress that, in their messy and precarious ways, have actually been achieved. And, as my paradigms show, some of those actual advances have been truly momentous.

are fruitful connections between the Deweyan pragmatism I elaborate in these lectures and the project undertaken by the Frankfurt School, especially as it is elaborated by Jaeggi and by Axel Honneth. In "John Dewey Goes to Frankfurt" (Julia Christ, Kristina Leopold, Daniel Loick, and Titus Stahl [eds.], *Debating Critical Theory: Engagements with Axel Honneth*, London: Rowman and Littlefield, 2020, 247–267), I attempt to make the linkage clear.

3

The Many Modes of Moral Progress

I

These lectures began with the search for an alternative to the Discovery View of moral progress. Now that my proposed rival has been presented, it is worth considering how it relates to the Discovery View. We can then examine how *both* positions need elaboration if they are to do justice to the varieties of moral progress.

Earlier I promised to explore a pragmatist approach to moral truth and moral discovery. The most famous pragmatist suggestion about truth stems from Peirce: "The opinion which is fated to be ultimately agreed to by all who investigate, is what we mean by the truth."[1] I prefer James's variant formulation, which sees the truth as what "is expedient" in the long run.[2] Thus, instead of thinking of truth as emerging in the limit of properly conducted collective inquiry, I shall view the true moral judgments as those statements about the rightness or wrongness of actions that would endure as the stable elements in a progressive moral practice, no matter how long it might be extended.[3]

Imagine, then, a human community that begins the moral project as I claim our ancestors initiated it, tackling, as they unwittingly did, the fundamental problem of our limited responsiveness to one another. Suppose them to employ the moral methods I have sketched to modify the judgments they make about how to act, and later about

---

[1] C. S. Peirce, "How to Make our Ideas Clear," in *Collected Papers of Charles Sanders Peirce*, Volumes V and VI, ed. Charles Hartshorne and Paul Weiss (Cambridge, MA: Harvard University Press, 1935).
[2] William James, *Pragmatism* (Cambridge, MA: Harvard University Press, 1975).
[3] James might be seen as replacing the idea of convergence to a limit with the Cauchy criterion for assessing convergence.

Philip Kitcher, *The Many Modes of Moral Progress* In: *Moral Progress*. Edited by: Jan-Christoph Heilinger, Oxford University Press. © Oxford University Press 2021. DOI: 10.1093/oso/9780197549155.003.0004

how to live. Whenever they begin, however long their lineage lasts, however their community expands or contracts, whatever social and physical innovations their efforts generate, some judgments will endure. These judgments count as the moral—and, more broadly, as the ethical—truths.

For there are some pervasive features of human life. We are social animals, with capacities for harming one another. In any context, human vulnerability entails that the problem of our limited responsiveness can only be addressed by introducing prohibitions against initiating violence. Our lives also depend on exchanging information. Thus arises a presumption in favor of truthfulness. Any human community pursuing the methods I've outlined will introduce and retain maxims against aggression and in favor of honesty. Those maxims are hard to state exactly, for they cannot be fully general. Sometimes responsiveness demands violent restraint of people who threaten the lives of others, or deceiving those who seek information in order to effect massive harm. Vague generalizations forbidding violence and enjoining honesty would appear to be stable elements in all the progressive moral communities we can imagine—and hence count as good candidates for moral truths.

The three examples on which I have drawn throughout these lectures seem to furnish further true moral judgments. It is wrong for people to own other people, wrong for women to be denied opportunities available to men, wrong to oppress those who have sexual relations with members of their own sex. Like the maxims concerning aggression and truthfulness, these judgments are imprecise. What are the boundaries of ownership? What physiological or psychological differences properly limit equality of opportunity? How far does oppression extend? Negative claims about what it is wrong to do are often articulated as positive requirements on conduct, creating a moral superstructure that typically depends on the institutions of a society and on the technologies at its disposal.

So, it appears, my approach can make sense of moral discovery. It can even endorse the central theme of the Discovery View. At the heart of the three moral revolutions I've considered were cognitive achievements. People discovered the wrongness of slavery, the wrongness of unequal treatment of men and women, and the wrongness of persecuting homosexuals. Is my supposed alternative really a version of the Discovery View after all?[4]

I think not. The significant difference between my approach and that of proponents of the Discovery View lies in disagreement about whether there is some prior "Moral Reality" that somehow prescribes to our conduct. Identifying the source of the divergence will require me to make some distinctions I have so far avoided.

On a superficial view, the gap between the two views looks obvious. Moral realists (Parfit, Scanlon, and Nagel, for example) take there to be something independent of human beings and their psychological lives that determines the rightness or wrongness of actions, or, perhaps, what people "have reason to do." Democratic contractualism, by contrast, emphasizes the interactions among people with different perspectives, how they advance beyond conflict to mutual understanding. Yet we should recall Peirce's ominous reference to what is "fated" to emerge, and the methodological constraints behind the notion of a progressive sequence of practices. My Jamesian approach would select as true those judgments that prove stable in the long run, *when the appropriate method of moral inquiry is followed*. Deliberations among groups of individuals only yield moral discoveries when they conform to the ideal moral methodology—when the group is inclusive and the participants are informed and mutually engaged. The ideal method seems to play the same role as the realist's "moral reality" or "realm of reason."

This rejoinder is genuinely insightful, for it discloses that mere reference to human negotiations doesn't suffice to break with a realist picture. At the same time, it imports into my alternative approach an alien element. For, as I have frequently remarked, the methodology I've presented is the first stage in an envisaged process through which methods of inquiry are to be revised, extended, and refined. My approach to moral truth characterized it as what emerges and is retained when *the method I have outlined here* is repeatedly applied. That formulation is overly simple and strictly incorrect, although useful as an introductory device, for I have anticipated methodology itself as

---

[4] Thanks to Wesley Holliday, Niko Kolodny, and Jay Wallace for raising penetrating—and different—versions of this question.

progressively evolving. As it does so, the stable elements generated from methods at earlier stages might be replaced at later stages by different stable elements. The truths we hail are thus doubly provisional, based not only on the past career of particular precepts but also on our current judgments about method in moral inquiry.

So what? Let's simply incorporate the progressive development of method in moral inquiry. The moral truths, then, are those featuring as stable elements in moral practice when that practice is indefinitely elaborated using the method attained at the ideal limit (call it the "Ideal Method.") Hence we re-establish the idea of a constraint that picks out some moral judgments as "fated to emerge," whatever deliberations human beings engage in. The contingencies of actual human discussions thus appear to be beside the point.

To elaborate the approach along those lines is to import into the picture just the teleological approach to progress I have been at pains to reject. Progress in moral methodology is being conceived in terms of increasing proximity to some fixed goal, an Ideal Method. In parallel to my treatment of moral progress as problem-solving, I view methodological progress in pragmatic terms. We advance our methods for inquiry by overcoming the problems that beset them and pushing back their limits.

At this point, an obvious worry arises. To make sense of pragmatic moral progress, it was necessary to identify problems and to say what counts as solving them. I tackled those tasks by developing an account of method in moral inquiry. Will the attempt to understand methodological progress in pragmatic terms generate similar demands, requiring a *meta*methodology? Am I launched on an infinite regress?

I think not. Methods for inquiry prove their worth by yielding conclusions that remain stable in the course of further inquiry. When we discover that our current methodology has licensed acceptance of judgments that are later reversed, it is worth asking if our methods can be amended to do better. Sometimes we can see no way of making superior use of the evidence at hand. On other occasions, however, methodological adjustment allows for greater systematic success. The sciences supply familiar examples. Medical researchers learned the value of double-blind testing.

Thinking of methodological progress as pragmatic progress alters the picture of moral truth. We should imagine a sequence of moral practices coupled with a sequence of maxims for moral inquiry. The moral practice at any stage is modified using the methods that have emerged at that stage, and those methods are continually assessed in terms of the successes and failures discernible in the history of moral practices—judged by the stability of the conclusions our methods endorse.

But now the notion of moral truth begins to appear far more nebulous than my earlier confident judgments about the inevitability of preserving certain kinds of maxims would have suggested. Endorsing a moral generalization—"It is typically right to tell the truth," say— appears to depend on anticipating what the future will bring as methods of moral inquiry we can only dimly foresee are brought to bear on situations and human complaints we struggle to imagine. Talk of moral truth starts to look far less helpful than was advertised, involving the kinds of extravagant speculations sober pragmatists should find unappealing. Peirce and James hoped to help people *use* the concept of truth.[5]

The remedy, I suggest, is to change the subject. Instead of asking for an account of moral truth, focus on when we are justified in identifying—*provisionally*—particular claims as moral truths and particular episodes as constituting moral discoveries. I return to a more basic theme in pragmatism. Hailing a claim as true announces a resolve to rely on it in decision-making. If a community holds that a particular moral judgment has resulted from an inquiry conducted in accordance with the methods it endorses, members of that community are justified in using that judgment to guide their actions. Consider, in this light, the moral verdicts I characterized as truths: unprovoked aggression is wrong, truth-telling is typically right, owning other people is wrong, discrimination against women and same-sex lovers is wrong. Assuming the methodology presented in these lectures, I'm justified in

---

[5] Peirce and James are often taken to be attempting to *define* the notion of truth. Both of them, however, explicitly endorse a traditional (correspondence) definition. Their dissatisfaction arises from a judgment that this definition is "empty" or unhelpful. The project of Peirce's seminal essay, "How to Make Our Ideas Clear," is to guide us in employing concepts whose available definitions present difficulties in application.

classing these judgments as moral truths, because, in each case, I can see how they issued from a process roughly in accord with my maxims for moral inquiry. They can justifiably serve in my future deliberations.

Do I expect them to survive indefinitely in the future of moral practice? Probably not. Because I can relate them to a preferred moral methodology, it's hard to envisage how they might need refinement or replacement. Yet I know my own fallibility. Future ventures in moral inquiry, in accordance with the methods I favor, might uncover situations calling for modification, perhaps through some reconceptualization I can't yet envisage.[6] Moreover, I recognize the crudity of my methodological proposals. Who can tell what the subsequent progress of method in moral inquiry might be? If I am asked to predict the long-term stability of these verdicts, I would rather dodge the question. It is hard for me to envisage how they might disappear, and yet I'm forced to acknowledge the possibility.

But why do I have to predict at all? Of most concern to me is the immediate future, in which I feel confident in relying on these judgments. Moreover, I suppose that, if difficulties emerge, the best strategy for coping with them would be to deploy whatever sorts of moral inquiry my methodology then approves. If revisions are needed, taking my current judgments seriously and using my preferred methods looks like a good road to finding better ones. In short, I don't have to worry about long-term stability. What I need is a license to identify some judgments as true, and to rely on them in my subsequent actions until there are grounds for revoking the license.

Looking into the past, I recognize particular episodes as culminating in the endorsement of moral claims resembling those I'm justified in counting as true. The recognition undergirds my taking these episodes to be processes of moral discovery. Moreover, imagining alternative possibilities for history, scenarios in which approximations to proper moral inquiry occur earlier, I justifiably suppose that the discoveries

---

[6] Here I apply to the moral case an insight elaborated by Kyle Stanford with respect to the history of science. Stanford's version of the pessimistic induction on the history of science emphasizes the ways in which apparently successful scientific theories tend to be replaced by (even more successful) theories whose concepts were beyond the horizons of the earlier researchers. See his *Exceeding Our Grasp* (New York: Oxford University Press, 2006).

could have happened well before they did. Owning people was always morally wrong.

These kinds of thought experiments incline me to wonder whether the contingent details of *when* moral inquiry is initiated might matter. At any number of stages in the past people might have inquired into the issue of slavery. Even if we suppose the (crude) methods I have outlined here, the particular forms of the sufferings of the slaves together with the diverse attitudes and beliefs expressed in sympathetic reactions to them might have affected the solution eventually adopted.[7] When the progress of moral methodology is recognized, there seems little basis for supposing that some single set of moral truths is likely to emerge and remain stable through the indefinitely extending, doubly progressive, future. The historical details concerning how and when moral inquiry is initiated might affect the judgments that emerge and the concepts on which they draw. Better simply to recognize our justification in adopting what the best available form of moral inquiry generates, and our rightly increasing confidence when moral claims remain stable across progressive transitions.

The picture I have painted (surely with too broad a brush) recapitulates an apparently puzzling idea common to James and Dewey: the vision of a world (or of a moral structure) that is always incomplete, coming into being through collective human decisions and actions. If friends of the Discovery View were to declare that this was always what they had in mind when they talked of whatever it is that determines what people "have reason to do," I should be happy to welcome them as allies and to sign on to this version of the Discovery View. But I should also be very surprised by the declaration.

---

[7] Under different institutional conditions, the conceptualization of slavery and the consequent diagnosis of its ills might have been radically different. So it is possible to envisage different moral communities who recognize one another as making similar changes at moments in their histories, who view those in the rival community as achieving some sort of insight in doing so, but who reject the idioms in which the other community describes its advances. They accumulate alternative sets of moral judgments they each count as true, and can find ways of partially translating one another, but find the rival scheme of classification odd, or even defective.

II

As I noted, the Discovery View oversimplifies—and so, too, does the approach I have offered. A discovery, or the recognition of a solution to a problem, may be *central* to moral progress. Yet there's more to moral progress than a change in attitude. Without a modification of conduct, no moral advance occurs. Small children may sincerely believe they ought to share, while remaining just as grabby whenever temptation to hog arises. Competitive male academics may be chastened by feminist criticism, coming to see their earlier behavior in professional discussions as displays of testosterone poisoning; nevertheless, in the heat of the debate, the old desires to dominate may win the day. Moral progress requires connected changes. Modifications of psychology and of action must both occur—and the two must be coupled.

Earlier, I referred to the entities about which progress judgments are made as "systems." My discussions of the three guiding examples of moral progress have been woefully vague about just what the systems involved are. The abolition of slavery, the expansion of opportunities for women, and the acceptance of same-sex love all involve *social* changes, effected by rough and inefficient approximations to *collective* use of moral method, and featuring *psychological* alterations in a scatter of *individuals*. To arrive at a more precise and structured account of what occurred, I shall introduce concepts of *individual moral practice* and *social moral practice*, and explore some of their interconnections. Before undertaking that task, however, it's useful to recognize some preliminary points. Much of what I say should apply whether or not you adopt the Discovery View or its pragmatist rival.

Plainly, the large social changes do not reveal unanimous change in belief on the part of all members of the pertinent society.[8] The American Civil War didn't conclude in a state in which all citizens believed that slavery was, and always had been, morally wrong. Perhaps a majority of Americans would have signed on to that judgment, but many would have resisted. Legal reforms prevented most resisters from acting on their beliefs. Institutional changes also exerted

---

[8] The discussion of the next four paragraphs was prompted by some insightful comments of John MacFarlane.

pressure on them, forcing them sometimes to behave and speak as if they endorsed the "official" view. Such amendments were, and still are, inadequate for eradicating all forms of racism.

Nor were the beliefs of many of those who accepted the wrongness of slavery generated from processes that approximated the ideal deliberations moral methodology commends. Possibly among a few pioneers—people like John Woolman or Anthony Benezet—the course of private reflections simulated something like a dialogue among mutually engaged and well-informed representatives of the various perspectives. Later abolitionists, Frederick Douglass and Henry Ward Beecher, were drawn into debates that probably enabled them to recognize how a methodologically more adequate conversation would go. From 1865 on, adult Americans divided into three classes: those whose belief-forming processes were sufficiently akin to those approved by moral method to justify their belief that slavery is wrong; those who believed in the wrongness of slavery on the testimony of moral authorities; and those who continued to resist abolitionism, and whose conduct was partially restrained by the decisions of the powerful.

Moral discoveries have this much in common with scientific discoveries. Things "become known." By whom? Four decades ago, the reality of anthropogenic global warming became accepted by the community of climate scientists through a social process conforming to the methods that community endorsed. Knowledge has since spread to millions of people, almost all of whom lack the expertise to assess the evidence for themselves. Others harbor contrary opinions. In this instance, as in that of Darwinian evolution, resistance to the expert consensus is apparent. The realities of anthropogenic climate change and of Darwinian evolution have "become known." That social claim represents a highly varied distribution of psychological states among individual people.

Once this point is appreciated, it should become clear how moral progress can occur in societies without any dramatic increase in the moral quality of individuals. Sometimes non-moral changes even ease the way for moral advances. Late nineteenth-century social arrangements exposed the myth that abolition would spell economic doom for prosperous Southerners. Margaret Sanger's dedication to

spreading information about contraception generated a new environment for considering opportunities for women. On both occasions,
hard choices gave way to much more comfortable decisions.

The fit between moral progress at the individual and the social levels
is thus looser and more complicated than it might easily be taken to
be. I shall now attempt a more systematic investigation of some of the
details.

III

Individuals make moral progress when they revise their moral beliefs
in ways governed by the methodological maxims I have presented (or
by the progressive successors to those maxims). But only when certain
conditions are in place. The new beliefs must play a role in superior
conduct. Those beliefs must be pertinent to the situations in which the
people find themselves. Old habits must be reshaped. New kinds of reflection must be undertaken when the circumstances call for stopping
to think.

I shall start with individual moral progress, deferring for the moment the harder case of moral advance at the societal level. The
simplest picture of individual moral practice, surely adopted in many
philosophical discussions, views moral beliefs as consciously invoked
in directing behavior. We think of people saying to themselves "I
should do A" (or something similar), and of that self-counseling
issuing in their doing A. The connection between the thought (A is to
be done) and the deed (A) comes about through the action of a separate
faculty—the will. Hence arises the idea of a two-component account
of moral practice. People have a set of beliefs about what to do (and
what not to do), B, and a capacity for acting on their beliefs, W. What
is done is then a product of both components. The simple objection
to thinking of moral practice as one-dimensional (beliefs alone) stems
from recognizing that, if the will is sufficiently weak—W consists of
dispositions to ignore whatever is in B—changes in moral belief will
generate no differences in behavior.

My apparently pedantic elaboration of a very straightforward idea is
useful in preparing the way for some of the complexities to follow. For

the moment, however, it suffices to note that, on the two-component approach, changes in individual moral practice take the form:

$$< B,W > \rightarrow < B^*,W^* >$$

This immediately brings home the possibility of two independent modes of moral progress. First, progressive changes in beliefs, in the presence of an unchanged will disposed to translate some beliefs (including some of the modified ones) into action, generates improved conduct. So, too, do changes in will, increasing the disposition to act in accordance with moral beliefs, even if the set of moral beliefs is unaltered. Strengthening the will is a mode of individual moral progress. People who consistently fail to perform the actions they recognize as right, when they find themselves in situations of a particular kind, make moral progress through becoming able to resist distraction or temptation. They used to say "I know I shouldn't . . . but just this once"—and it wasn't just once, but a regular feature of that sort of circumstance. Now, in the same circumstances, they know they shouldn't—and they don't. Background beliefs haven't changed, but they have become morally stronger.

The everyday notion of strength of will can be captured by thinking about all the situations in which agents find themselves. That large class can be partitioned into two subsets. The *positive* situations are those in which the moral belief is effective in action. The *negative* situations are those where it isn't. Strength of will is measured by the extent to which the set of positive situations is greater than the set of negative situations. Or, perhaps, by some more subtle index, taking into account the frequency with which situations arise and the consequences of the moral lapses (should we call them "moral holidays"?). In any event, transfer of some types of situations from negative to positive, without other alterations in will, would seem to constitute a mode of individual moral progress.

Sometimes a transition in individual moral practice modifies both beliefs and strength of will: $B \neq B^*$, and $W \neq W^*$. If the changes along both dimensions are progressive, there initially appears to be no problem in counting the whole as a progressive shift.[9] However, a

---

[9] Even here, however, matters are more complicated. Suppose that, on the whole, the new beliefs accord better with the methodological maxims than the old ones did.

progressive shift in one component may be accompanied by regress in the other. Consider someone who becomes more sympathetic, no longer reacting harshly to the foibles of others. Perhaps, after reading *War and Peace*, she accepts the advice given to Prince Andrew by his sister, Maria—"*Tout comprendre c'est tout pardonner*"—and she starts to enter into the situations of others. But this commendable shift goes along with a tendency to forgive herself in succumbing to particular kinds of temptations. As she indulges herself, she is reassured by the thought that people shouldn't be as strict as she used to be. Of course, the combination of progress on one dimension and regress on the other can also involve strengthening the will at cost to progress in moral beliefs. Dedication to the idea of becoming stricter in one's moral life can bring about rigidity and harshness toward others. When these kinds of changes combine, overall verdicts about moral progress are often unclear. It's no accident that the validity of the (probably ancient) maxim Tolstoy puts into Maria's mouth has been vigorously debated.

So far, so elementary. Indeed, much too elementary. Stopping at two components will not do. Consider these cases.

(1) There are situations in which a person is consciously aware of a moral directive she accepts, but in which she wonders whether that directive is really applicable to the current circumstances.

(2) There are situations in which a person is consciously aware of a moral directive she accepts but also aware of other parts of her corpus of moral beliefs that point toward alternative courses of action. The extreme case of this is when she recognizes that she has contradictory moral beliefs.

(3) There are situations in which a person is consciously aware of a moral directive she accepts but also doubts whether the

---

Assume, too, that the will becomes stronger across a wider set of beliefs. It remains possible for the strengthening of the will to affect responses primarily to beliefs that are *not* sanctioned by the maxims. The net result is to increase the percentage of contexts in which morally dubious behavior occurs. More generally, there can be interaction effects among components of moral practice. I am grateful to Sebastian Watzl for leading me to appreciate these possibilities.

concepts in terms of which that directive is framed are the right ones.

(4) There are situations in which a person is puzzled about what to do. Canvassing her stock of moral beliefs, she finds that none of them offers any clear direction for acting in the current circumstances.

(5) There are situations (many situations!) in which a person acts in a way that has moral implications, and she does so without considering the rightness of what she does.

Cases (1)–(3) are cases of *moral conflict*. Case (4) typifies *moral incompleteness*. Cases (1)–(4) are all proper starting points for moral inquiry. Case (5) covers cases of *moral habit*. A large majority of these latter cases should *not* be starting points for moral inquiry. (We cannot live by suspending judgment, postponing action, and investigating everything.)

Examples of the various types are easy to come by. For Case (1), we need only imagine a person accosted by a beggar, whose unkempt appearance excites her sympathy. She believes that she should help the needy and downtrodden (the parable of the Good Samaritan is salient for her). Yet the beggar's spasmodic gestures and haggard expression give her pause. It would be easy to give a small amount of money. But she wonders, reasonably, what use would be made of her gift. Would it go toward the next fix? Lacking the opportunity to hand over food or water, she doesn't know what to do.

To illustrate Case (2), imagine someone deeply committed to a political cause, involved with helping immigrants to her country who have fled persecution at home. She spends considerable time in efforts to help these refugees adapt to their new environment. As she is engaged in this work, a political movement, dedicated to restricting immigration, imposing stringent conditions on permanent asylum, and so forth, grows in strength. Like others who are trying to help the newcomers, she now devotes some of her energy to resistance against the anti-migrant movement, participating in debates and public forums. The clashes between the rival groups become ever more marked by violent rhetoric (and occasional veiled threats of physical assault) on the part of her opponents. Our protagonist firmly believes in calm attempts at engagement with others, but she is increasingly aware of her lack of success when she follows the peaceful course her principles favor. So she begins to wonder whether the only way to pursue the good she intends—the protection of the refugees—is to resort to more aggressive ways of responding to the people who want to expel them.

For Case (3), imagine an elderly woman whose moral views have responded to large social changes. During her lifetime, she has come to accept different ideas about the possible roles for women from those she was taught in her youth. She has also overcome her initial prejudices about homosexual relations. These changes have given her a sense of the need for sympathy with human beings whose ways of life initially seemed strange, disturbing, and even repellent. As the existence of transgender people in her society, and in her local community, becomes ever clearer to her, she wants to build on the lessons about engagement with the perspectives of others that she has learned. Yet, as she tries to decide what she should say and do in specific contexts, she is painfully aware that the language available to her is unsuited to her interactions with transgender people. Although she tries to explore writings about gender, she finds what she reads opaque. Her actions are inhibited (and, she realizes, often stiff) because she doesn't have the concepts to develop the kinds of sympathy and understanding she would like to acquire and to express.

Our protagonist has also paid attention to the planet's changing climate. She is convinced that the world is warming and that human beings are the principal causes of the increase in average global temperature. She recognizes that the consequences for future generations are likely to be severe. But she is also aware of the plight of many people in her own country, as well as the vast majority of the citizens of the poorer nations. As she thinks about the changes that are needed, and about the various proposals that are made, she finds it impossible to assess them. She appreciates the need to mitigate the sufferings of future people who would otherwise live in a much harsher environment but also the need to address the deprivations felt by vast numbers of presently living human beings. Moreover, she appreciates the cultural and political achievements of the human past, and she is reluctant to sacrifice them to improve the basic conditions of existence. She canvasses her moral beliefs in vain. They offer her no advice on how to balance the competing demands. Her predicament aligns with Case (4).

Case (5) has been made famous by Bernard Williams, in his story of the husband who plunges in to save his drowning wife. It's also illustrated by actual examples. Wesley Autrey leapt onto the New York subway tracks, saving a passenger who had fallen by using his body to cover, while the train passed over them both. Magda Trocmé opened her arms to a young Jewish child who had sought refuge in her home in Vichy France, saying immediately, "Come in, come in." Habit pervades our conduct.[10] We undertake our daily routines without thinking, not wondering about whether we should set out for work, or greet those we meet, or concentrate on the tasks we are supposed to fulfill, or buy lunch for a friend, or propose an evening's entertainment, or whatever. Sometimes those habitual actions are morally exactly right; on other occasions they are not.

How people react to these kinds of situations depends on capacities of a particular type. I shall call them *sensitivities*. The most fundamental kind of sensitivity is one that differentiates cases in which proceeding by habit (doing the routine thing) is justified from cases in which some reflection is required. Here, as elsewhere, the methodology presented in earlier sections sets the standard of justification: operating by habit is allowed just where an ideal discussion would permit it. As noted earlier, people go astray in two different ways, sometimes plunging ahead when they ought to stop and reflect, sometimes dithering, Hamlet-like, when they should act decisively. Human sensitivity to habit—S_H—is imperfect. It provides another dimension along which individuals can make moral progress.

This sensitivity covers a number of subordinate sensitivities. For the ways in which habits are set up in us depend on our reactions to our experiences. Likewise, how we act when habitual practice is checked by the need for reflection is the product of other psychological capacities and dispositions. I'll begin with the formation and consolidation of habits.

---

[10] This point is central to Dewey's most extensive discussion of moral psychology; see *Human Nature and Conduct* (*Middle Works*, Volume 14).

The habits pervading our daily conduct are largely shaped by the social milieu in which we develop and live. How could it be otherwise? To think of our moral practices as built up entirely from scratch, through our own efforts, is as absurd as the analogous fiction about our factual beliefs. There is a social analog of individual moral practice, something that represents the concepts, beliefs, and approaches to behavior current in our society (or community), from which our practices draw. In part, the transfer from what is socially accepted to the practices of individuals is achieved through education (in the institutionalized way in which education is normally viewed), but it is surely not restricted to what people learn in classrooms. Education, including moral education, in a broader sense, begins in interactions with parents, caregivers, and siblings, and continues throughout our lives in our observations of the actions of others and in their responses to and appraisals of what we do. Often, the habits guiding daily conduct conform to those of which the ambient society approves. We learn "what is done" by the people around us, and, without much reflection, we do the same, sometimes day by day, throughout our lives.

It would be hard to deny a sense in which the habits produced by imitative learning are justified. Once the impossibility of building a moral practice by ourselves is acknowledged, some exercises in emulation are inevitable parts of habit formation. Yet most of us (at least beyond a certain age) learn painfully that some of the habits we have acquired, relatively automatically by conforming to the patterns of behavior we see in those around us, need to be discarded. Vocabulary learned in our youth turns out to cause offense, and, with a sense of shame, we wean ourselves from it. A stronger standard of justification would invoke the methodology I have outlined. A habit is justified when it would be endorsed by participants in an ideal conversation. This more rigorous notion of justification cannot, however, crowd out its weaker relative. To come to be able to recognize what the more stringent standards would require, human beings need to be already immersed in moral practice. Nor is it ever feasible for any of us to undertake some Cartesian moral retreat, in which all our acquired habits are suspended and we reflect on which ones would survive in the court of ideal deliberation. For there is no way of pursuing the envisaged reflections without employing some—indeed many—of the habits we have acquired.

So I shall say that the habits formed by picking up elements of the ambient moral culture—the *social moral practice*, as I shall call it—are weakly justified. In imitating the approved behavior of our elders and of our peers, people tacitly see themselves as consolidating the moral achievements of the past. The tradition into which they are born has settled particular features of moral life. Those aspects can be taken for granted, allowing the moral agent to expend energy on the difficult situations that arise. Of course, some human beings develop habits contrary to those of which their society approves. They may be unobservant, or lazy, or strongly moved by impulses at odds with the favored habits—or simply unlucky in the sample of conduct they experience. From the perspective of weak justification, these people have formed bad habits. Nevertheless, on occasion (probably very rarely), the "bad habits" might turn out to be approved in an ideal deliberation. It is thus possible (although not likely) for a habit to be strongly justified but weakly unjustified.[11] As we shall see later, this possibility opens up dimensions along which transitions in *social* moral practice may be progressive.

The transaction between social and individual practice can go poorly in several ways. Using language familiar from other educational contexts, the pupil may be maladroit or the teacher incompetent. Concentrate for the present on the foibles of individuals. As already noted, people can be poor at recognizing the kinds of habits of which their society approves, or stubborn in resisting potential habits they find confining. Psychological capacities and dispositions underlie the shortcomings and the corresponding virtues. We can recognize two derivative sensitivities: *observational* sensitivity and *formational* sensitivity (S_O and S_F). Consequently there are two further types of individual moral progress, when people become more perceptive of the patterns of behavior approved in their societies and when they become

---

[11] Something similar occurs in the case of some great scientific revolutionaries, who contravene the methodological maxims of their age, advancing hypotheses that eventually, when embedded in a new (improved) methodology, become accepted. Galileo is perhaps the most obvious example.

more disposed to acquire the approved patterns they perceive (they become more obedient).

The distinction between strong and weak justification should make it clear that these virtues must be balanced by other sensitivities. If societies are to throw off the bad habits they have inculcated in their members, at least some of the members should be prepared from time to time to question their ingrained patterns of conduct. Each of my paradigms of moral progress depended on the propensity of people to question routine behavior they and their fellows had taken for granted. John Woolman might easily have acceded automatically to his employer's request, and thought nothing of signing the document transferring ownership of a slave. Instead, he began to worry about participating in a process commonly viewed as part of everyday living. His reservations exemplify two important sensitivities: a willingness to reflect on entrenched parts of the dominant moral code, coupled with a recognition of which parts of the code merited extended consideration. Because of these sensitivities, Woolman began moral inquiry and was thus led to begin a campaign for abolishing slavery. Another dimension of moral practice consists in sensitivity to places at which moral inquiry might be initiated (S_I), with a correlative type of moral progress achieved through improvements of that sensitivity.

Sometimes, in situations where some contrary impulse interrupts the smooth operation of a habit, explicit consideration of the accepted set of moral judgments will resolve the tension. A feature of our circumstances makes us suddenly tentative in going on as we normally would have done. We stop to reflect, asking how our stock of moral beliefs bears on the case at hand. There are two different possible outcomes. Perhaps the appeal to our moral beliefs settles the issue. They offer firm guidance, either for continuing the established routine or for forsaking habit in the present instance. Alternatively, we find ourselves at a loss. Canvassing our moral beliefs, we become convinced that the opposition between impulse and habit corresponds to a tension among them. Or maybe, as we reflect, we appreciate that nothing in our antecedent beliefs has prepared us for this particular situation. Confused about how to go on, we do what Woolman did: we begin a moral investigation.

The sensitivity involved in starting moral inquiry (S_I) is thus interwoven with further sensitivities: a capacity for using our established moral beliefs in responding to conditions in which we are brought up short (S_U) and a capacity for undertaking moral inquiry in ways that are likely to yield progress. The latter capacity should conform, at least approximately, to the methodological maxims of previous sections. It therefore depends on our abilities to simulate the course of ideal discussion: including capacities for representing the perspectives of those who would be affected by the actions viewed as options, our capacities for engaging with those perspectives, and our factual knowledge. There are thus three subsidiary sensitivities: sensitivity to perspectives (S_P), sensitivity in engaging with those perspectives (S_E), and sensitivity to the available information about features of the world pertinent to identifying consequences (S_K). Improvements in any of these sensitivities constitute modes of moral progress.

Enough! I have multiplied sensitivities to the point of caricature in order to make some important points. We began with the recognition that moral progress is not simply a matter of acquiring better moral beliefs. That inspired a two-dimensional model of moral change, in which moral beliefs and strength of will marked out two dimensions. It should now be clear that two dimensions are woefully inadequate. Consideration of scenarios of Cases (1)–(5) leads to a more intricate and more adequate "model" that might be set down—with triumphant pedantry—as follows:

$$< B, W, S_H, S_O, S_F, S_I, S_U, S_P, S_E, S_K > \rightarrow < B^*, W^*, S_H{}^*, S_O{}^*, S_F{}^*, S_I{}^*, S_U{}^*, S_P{}^*, S_E{}^*, S_K{}^* >$$

Moral progress is now seen in terms of advances along any of the ten dimensions, so long as the gains are not offset by losses on one or more of the others.[12]

---

[12] The multidimensional approach to progress envisaged here parallels some of my earlier thoughts about progress in the natural sciences (see Chapter 4 of *The Advancement of Science* [New York: Oxford University Press, 1993]). Although I have modified my views about how to identify the relevant dimensions, and how they should be characterized, I continue to believe that any adequate account of scientific progress must acknowledge the multidimensionality of practice.

Something of this sort is probably correct, but it would be ludicrous to hail the representation just displayed as the final account of individual moral practice—or even as a serious improvement on the two-dimensional model. The representation is a first effort at capturing aspects of individual moral life with respect to which progress might be made. It is generated from reflecting on particular types of scenarios, embedding them within a psychological framework derived from introspection (a "folk psychological" diagnosis of what occurs in specific cases.) Any adequate model must accommodate the phenomena—the scenarios that outrun the two-dimensional account. *How* that is to be done depends on the form of a serious psychological reconstruction. It is likely to be multidimensional in that it will identify independent capacities involved in moral practice (I suspect a fair number of them), but it may use a very different taxonomy, splitting some distinctions I have drawn and blurring others. Further, there is every reason to think that the list of cases out of which my cartoon model is generated is incomplete. What is offered, then, is a crude attempt to indicate the kinds of complexities that a psychologically informed picture of moral practice would have to introduce.

IV

In highlighting the notion of habit, the (preliminary) account I have offered draws attention to the ways in which social moral practice shapes the moral lives of individuals. Elaborating that connection through a multidimensional approach expands the educational possibilities. All too often, moral education is conceived as an exercise in inculcating beliefs—possibly supplemented by discipline to strengthen the will. The methodology of previous sections encourages projects designed to make moral deliberation go better. It suggests experimental programs introduced to help young people interact productively with others who are very different from themselves. Greater willingness to be inclusive and to engage with many perspectives might be stimulated by forming small groups of children to work together in planning activities, and gradually expanding the size of the group and the range of attitudes within it. Here, the aim would be to instill dispositions enabling people to do better at satisfying the conditions of an ideal conversation than they otherwise would. Understanding the finer grain of moral practice through recognizing the various kinds of sensitivities that might progressively be developed should inspire more specific exercises and activities. Educators ought to consider ways in which people might be brought to reflect on their habits, to use various kinds of moral resources (including the ideas assembled in various moral traditions—conceived now as tools for moral thinking rather than as rigid prescriptions), and to rehearse, in imagination, the ways in which inclusive, informed, and engaged deliberation would go. As Dewey saw, works of literature can play a major role in developing the powers of moral imagination.[13] So, too, can recognition of the course of historical responses to the "cries of the wounded" and detailed ethnographies that acquaint young people with very different forms of life. Even a cartoon model of moral practice can indicate avenues along which educational improvements might be sought. I explore these avenues elsewhere.[14]

Education (broadly construed) provides the most obvious link between individual moral practices and the "something" that makes up the moral code of the society. Any fully realistic treatment of moral practice must acknowledge that the entities we label "societies" contain a multiplicity of moral codes. At the highest level, perhaps, something is recognized by all the members of the society. Under this are various levels at which, as they descend, more is shared among those people (a decreasing number) who form communities, subcommunities, and so on. Even though the highest level imposes constraints on some aspects of socialization—through its specifications on allowable programs of formal education, for example—different local groups provide alternative patterns for their young members. I conjecture that this hierarchical structure varies across societies, both in the number of levels and in the demands imposed at the different levels. Consequently,

---

[13] See the final chapter of *Experience and Nature* (*Later Works*, Volume 1).

[14] In *The Main Enterprise of the World: Rethinking Education*, an expanded version of my Walter A. Strauss Lectures, presented at Case Western University in December 2017, (New York: Oxford University Press, 2021). See especially Chapters 5 and 9.

I doubt whether any useful model of social moral practice (one that goes beyond vague banalities) can be general and also accurate.

Hence, I shall idealize, considering the simplest case. There is one social level that interacts with the moral practices of individuals. The idealization is not pointless. For it can expose the social functions that need to be performed, however they are distributed and discharged among some number of hierarchical levels.

Social moral practice impinges on the members of a society in their education and continues to constrain individual moral practices through the system of laws and conventions for "acceptable behavior." It supplies the young with a language for discussing questions about how to act. This language may not only contain terms for "thick" moral concepts, to which other cultures give different emphases (or none at all)—think of *chaste, magnanimous, cruel, manly, convivial*—but also have a distinctive vocabulary for fundamental moral appraisal. In various societies, "evil," "pious," "proper," "honorable," and "vicious," have all played this role. Indeed, some groups have used their own name as the term of approval for conduct; instead of goodness or rightness, they talk of "what we do."

Within this language, the people approved as educators will formulate a number of statements that members of the society are to accept and use for moral guidance. Some of these are general principles—commandments—specifying how to act across a range of situations. Others endorse—or repudiate—the patterns of behavior exemplified by various figures, mostly historical or mythical. An important part of moral education consists in presenting exemplars of the conduct to be imitated or to be avoided. The presentations frequently consist in stories, parables, or narratives purporting to be history.

New members also need to learn about the institutions of their society. At the most general level, they have to understand differences among various domains of human life—how, for example, marriage, war, and financial transactions affect what is to be done and not done. They must grasp (at least in part) the relations among moral requirements, legal requirements, religious duties, and matters of etiquette. Within the institutions associated with different domains, they have to distinguish among roles and recognize the particular demands placed upon those who occupy the roles. An important part of social moral practice consists in accepting an organization of social life and thereby opposing some types of deviation from that order.

The social moral practice may do more. It may identify some moral matters as so firmly settled that they no longer need questioning and thus encourage consolidation of particular habits. By contrast, it can explicitly recognize some types of situations as unsettled and thus call for moral reflection. It can offer a methodology for moral inquiry, perhaps one that favors consulting particular types of people or particular texts.

So far, then, a picture of social moral practice as a multidimensional entity, some of whose components correspond to the dimensions of individual moral practices, emerges:

$$< L, B, O, H, U, M >$$

Here, the moral beliefs (B), the matters regarded as firmly settled and thus as suitable for habitual behavior (H), correlate quite directly with components of individual practice. The language (L) might be introduced into individual practice as well, although it seems less salient at the individual level. The unsettled questions (U) have a counterpart in the sensitivities associated with suspending the operation of habit, and the methodology (M) is loosely related to the specific sensitivities for conducting moral inquiry. The social organization (O) has no obvious analog in individual practice.

I believe that the model of social moral practice just outlined delineates the structure shared by the moral codes of almost all the human societies that have existed. They have, of course, varied greatly in their development of the components and in the ways they have implemented the tasks arising from the corresponding educational functions. (Some societies have given very explicit guidance on how unsettled moral questions are to be resolved; many societies have distributed the transmission of accepted moral lore among more or less inclusive groups.) In light of the picture I have given, it's easy to make sense of progress along each of the dimensions. Most obvious are the replacement of the prevalent moral beliefs by modifying them in light of my proposed methodology and, of course, substituting that methodology for whatever occupies the methodological component of the practice. Slightly less apparent is the reform of language to facilitate use of the precepts transmitted, both in action and in deliberation. Judgments about which parts of the accepted moral corpus count as achievements of the past, so firmly established that they can now safely be consolidated as habits, can be amended so as to achieve a better channeling of moral energy, enabling people to concentrate on the hard cases that confront them. Improvements in identifying classes of unsettled questions can relieve the burden on individual decisions about whether situations call for reflection. Adjustments of the social organization to accord with the moral beliefs would also constitute progressive shifts.

Yet these are not the only modes of social-level moral progress. The insufficiency of the picture presented so far embodies a point made at the very beginning of these lectures. The model applies to societies that regard their moral practice as final, extremely conservative traditions convinced that any change would be corruption—or to societies whose moral progress is contingent and haphazard. For, so far, the link between social practice and the practices of individuals has been viewed in terms of socialization, via a process in which the accomplishments of the past have been transmitted to the next generation. I have not identified any channel for a contrary motion, from the moral deliberations of individuals or of groups to a progressive revision of social moral practice. *Perhaps* there have been some societies, probably relatively recent, in which the potential need for moral reform has been appreciated. Those societies (assuming there are any) are the exceptions to my conjecture that the six-dimensional version applies generally.

I suggest that adding further dimensions of social moral practice is crucial to fostering systematic reform. If the Deweyan attempt to make moral progress more systematic and sure-footed is to succeed, social moral practice must already embody explicitly the need for scrutiny of the six components I have specified, with an eye to how advances might be made. A threefold division of societies proves useful here. *Rigidly conservative* societies do not amend their social moral practices. However individuals modify their moral practices during the course of their lives—regardless of whether a large number, or even all the people, make the same changes—the socialization of the next generation remains unaltered. *Haphazardly progressive* societies do better than this, by allowing some of the trends in the individual modifications in practice to be registered in the social practice, and thus to affect the education of later generations. *Deweyan* societies take a further step. Aware of the possibilities of moral progress, they take steps to encourage exploration of possible improvements and to incorporate some of the resultant changes into social practice.

How might that be done? Through institutional mechanisms for promoting change and for evaluating the kinds of changes made. In a Deweyan society, it is a commonplace that the beliefs acquired by individual members might admit of refinement, that the consolidated habits might require changing, and that the organization of society might be improved.[15] Of course, the Deweyan society takes its current moral practice seriously. Nevertheless, it encourages some of its members to think about alternatives. Nothing is so firmly settled as to be sacrosanct (not even the Deweyan commonplace itself!). Yet, while inquiry into the status of accepted beliefs, familiar habits, and social organization is fostered, the results of such inquiry are not immediately translated into action. In the Deweyan society, critical questioning is regarded favorably, but, unless the answers proposed by the critics have been duly assessed *in accordance with the favored version of moral methodology*, the critics are not justified in translating their putative findings into action. A claimed reform should not lead to modified conduct until its progressiveness is shown to be justified. If the Deweyan society is a version of our own, that means the revision should accord with the methodological maxims I have outlined. It must be endorsed by an ideal conversation among representatives of all those who would be affected by it.

The Deweyan society will also recognize that progressive reforms can be incomplete. As my paradigms reveal, a progressive change in moral beliefs may not realize its full potential because the discarded

---

[15] These are central themes of Chapter 6 of *Experience and Nature* (*Later Works*, Volume 1). When Dewey turns to discuss questions about the mind, his first interest is not in any version of the traditional mind-body problem. He is far more concerned to understand how societies can combine socializing all citizens, so as to allow the cohesion on which healthy social life depends, with fostering the development of "individual minds" that might spark progressive moral and social change.

ideas remain embedded in roles and institutions. Thus the Deweyan society will attempt to go beyond a merely superficial modification of the belief component of social moral practice. It will try to understand the ways in which rejected conceptions linger in social organization and, on this basis, modify pertinent aspects of that organization. Social experimentation will usually be necessary to carry this out effectively.

Hence my six dimensions of social moral practice are not enough. There must be (at least) a seventh, consisting in the practical procedures through which a Deweyan society encourages social critique, through which it limits the effects of changes proposed by critics until they have been scrutinized, through which it applies its moral methodology to the assessment of suggested reforms, and through which it searches out the places in which officially repudiated ideas may continue to affect conduct. My initial aim of making moral progress more systematic and sure-footed thus culminates in advocating a new cluster of social institutions. Those institutions are charged with identifying places that seem ripe for moral progress and educating a cadre of critics who might contribute proposals for further advances. In short, the Deweyan society needs philosophers—Deweyan philosophers, that is.

If our own society were to move in a Deweyan direction, there are many steps it might take. Individually or collectively, people might try to apply the moral methodology to difficult cases. Education might foster the ability of all citizens to engage in and to imagine ideal deliberations.[16] Groups might be convened to focus on the largest and most recalcitrant problems. While every member of the society might be encouraged to think critically about the status quo, particular individuals—Deweyan philosophers—might emerge as particularly talented in identifying good topics for discussion, offering promising proposals for reform, and mediating the society-wide deliberations.

Hence my account of social moral progress leads to serious tasks for education and for designing social institutions that will pursue moral inquiry in a less haphazard way.

---

[16] As I have suggested in *The Main Enterprise of the World*. See note 14 earlier.

V

These lectures began with regretful sympathy for the failure of our predecessors to recognize things that now seem completely evident. It is only just that they end with brief thoughts about our own blind spots. What might *we* be missing?

There are four possibilities:

1. The dulling of sensitivities in a globally connected world. Although our actions have long-range consequences, they lie beyond our purview. We are located in a vast network, and our habits are tuned by the perceived impact on the nodes adjacent to us.

2. The failure to provide resources so that people can realize the ideals supposedly promised to them. Philosophical reflection often assumes that education helps the young discover their own talents and, on this basis, make autonomous choices of a satisfying pattern for their lives. It further supposes that people will have sufficient support to pursue their chosen trajectories successfully. For the vast majority of human beings, even in the more affluent societies, these assumptions combine in a cruel joke.

3. The emphasis on economic productivity generates debased versions of ideals of the self. Instead of fostering projects that might genuinely improve the lives of others, human effort is channeled into ventures of no lasting significance. The supposedly "satisfying life" becomes one defined by the acquisition and consumption of material goods and social status. In a further twist, a large proportion of the human population is doomed to fail to realize even the bastardized version of the ideal.

4. The stark competition taken to be crucial to economic productivity erodes the community structures within many societies. Thus the opportunities for framing and pursuing genuinely satisfying ideals of the self—those dedicated to positive connections with the lives of others—are reduced. What is often advertised as an advance beyond hedonism destroys the conditions under which communal hedonism—the most fruitful ideal in the

previous history of our species—can flourish. The alleged advance would better be seen as a retreat.

It would be premature to declare outright that these features of the present age are analogous to the sources of trouble found in my paradigms. They do, however, give rise to a clear and definite moral problem.

Unless the human population radically changes its ways during the immediate future, our descendants are highly likely to inhabit a world so harsh and inhospitable as to challenge and confine their lives. Yet climate action is—quite reasonably—resisted by a large number of people who recognize how the measures proposed to curb the warming of our planet would make their own precarious predicaments even more difficult. The contemporary human population continually fails to grapple with a multisided dilemma.[17] How are we to cut the emissions of greenhouse gases so as to avoid threatening the lives of our descendants, while simultaneously attending to the legitimate aspirations of developing nations, ameliorating the condition of the world's poor, and preserving the valuable accomplishments of the human past? That is, I suggest, the most critical moral problem of our times. It requires moral inquiry, pursued by the methods I have tried to sketch, and, in my judgment, that inquiry must explore the four features toward which I have gestured.

We, too, have failed to hear the cries of the wounded. Many of them are already living, in distant places all over the globe; others are suffering close to home. Far, far more cannot call out to us directly, because they are not yet born. If we do not open our imaginations and try to listen for their reproaches, they may well lack the strength to cry at all.

---

[17] For elaboration of this point, see Philip Kitcher and Evelyn Fox Keller, *The Seasons Alter: How to Save Our Planet in Six Acts* (New York: W.W. Norton [Liveright], 2017), especially 165–173.

COMMENTS

The Limits of Conversation

Amia Srinivasan

1.

One of the things I like so much about all of Philip's work is how seriously it takes the idea of philosophy as a part of the humanities. This is on display in these Munich Lectures on moral progress, not least in Philip's striking call for moral philosophers to attend more carefully to history. Indeed, I think one way of seeing Philip's project is as a call for moral philosophers to stop taking scientific progress as our model for moral progress, and to instead take seriously the models of moral progress we already find in the study of history. Such a historical inquiry would give us, Philip suggests, a theory of moral progress that would not merely explain its possibility, but moreover hasten its occurrence, making moral progress "more sure-footed."

On Kitcher's view, what we find when we look at actual histories of moral progress are narratives of moral and political change that fit poorly with the "Discovery View." These historical narratives, Kitcher says, offer no account of how it is that the activities that participants in moments of moral change undertake—reflection, debate, consciousness-raising, organizing, protest—help them get onto the (putatively) objective moral truths. By contrast, historians of science do explain, or at least, Kitcher says, "presuppose," a parallel account of how scientific activity generates knowledge of the objective scientific truths. So while histories of scientific theory change lend credence to the Discovery View of *scientific* progress, histories of moral change cast doubt on the Discovery View of moral progress.

Amia Srinivasan, *The Limits of Conversation* In: *Moral Progress*. Edited by: Jan-Christoph Heilinger, Oxford University Press. © Oxford University Press 2021. DOI: 10.1093/oso/9780197549155.003.0005

But I am not yet convinced that Kitcher is right here. It is, of course, true that very few historians offer anything like a full-blown metaethics, explaining just why it is, for example, that coming face to face with the actual conditions of slavery might conduce to knowledge of its evils. But the same is true for most historians of science and historians of mathematics. *They* simply take for granted that there is a connection between the procedures of scientific and mathematical inquiry and the delivery of scientific and mathematical truth, without generally taking sides on the debate about scientific or mathematical realism. If *we* are less puzzled by how Mendel's experiments with pea plants generate knowledge of the properties of genes than we are by how the feminist consciousness-raising groups of the 1970s were able to reveal the dynamics of patriarchal oppression, that is our problem, and not a problem raised by the historians. For historians of moral progress do tell us how it is that agents come to see behind ideological appearance through to the normative reality: they talk of Damascene moments and slow conversions, of confrontations with a shifting material reality, of the acquisition of new hermeneutical resources, of affective engagement with alternative perspectives, and of political crises that give rise to new forms of life. That is to say, when Kitcher finds in histories of moral progress no account of the mechanism by which moral truths are discovered, what he is really finding is his own antecedent skepticism about the Discovery View.

This is not to say that there are no epistemological puzzles about our access to objective moral truth. There are indeed profound puzzles here. Kitcher asks how it is that a pioneering abolitionist such as John Woolman was able to see that chattel slavery needed to be rejected, while others with similar experiences and backgrounds were not. Kitcher asks, "How was Woolman able to see what they missed?" This is a question we can generalize across space and time, to every person who has had moral insight where her peers have failed to see. In virtue of what are such people, we might call them moral prophets, able to see beyond the rest of us?

There are presumably complicated stories to be told here, at once structural—about the objective material relationship that such people have to systems of oppression—and highly personal: about the particular virtues of sensitivity and ethical creativity with which certain people are endowed. But do we really want to doubt that there are such people, who see more deeply and sensitively than others, just because we lack a satisfying account of what makes for such a person?

I think that the real source of Kitcher's worry here is his conviction that the Discovery View of moral progress, to be plausible, must be accompanied by a set of procedures for discovering the moral truth—procedures that can be operationalized by all agents regardless of their particular circumstances or backgrounds. Thus he writes that "The mysteries [of the Discovery View] would be dissolved if it became possible to see how the procedures conducive to moral discovery were followed by the participants on one side of an issue, and not by those on the other." Kitcher thinks that proponents of the Discovery View can offer us no such procedures, and that histories of moral progress show us that no such procedures exist: that people who are equally reasonable and equally well-intentioned end up on different sides of history.

But I think this is to misread history. One thing that the history of moral progress (such as it is) teaches us is that "being reasonable" and being well-intentioned are *not* procedures for getting onto the moral truth. (Another thing it teaches us is just how often the recognition of moral truths is contingent on progressive shifts in social practice, rather than the other way around.) In order to see a moral truth that is not generally recognized, one needs to be more than just reasonable or well-intentioned: one needs to be endowed with moral sensitivity, to be exposed to the right material occasions for exercising that sensitivity, to be equipped with the right hermeneutical resources or the creative ability to generate such resources, and to be endowed with the independence of mind to insist on describing the world as few others see it. Unlike being reasonable or being well-intentioned, being so endowed largely does not lie within an agent's control: it is in large part a matter of good luck. What the history of moral progress challenges is not the Discovery View, but the liberal fantasy that we are all equally equipped to get onto the moral truth, regardless of where we find ourselves in the space of social possibility. It also challenges the view, common to philosophers of all metaethical persuasions, that the key to moral change is ideological (a matter of better beliefs) rather than material (a matter of better practices).

If all this makes the search for moral truth different from the search for scientific truth, so be it. Such a difference needn't undermine the Discovery View of moral progress. It just shows us that what is involved in discovering moral truth is different from what is involved in discovering scientific truth. In other words, I think Kitcher's worries about the Discovery View of moral progress come from a false presupposition that morality, if objective, must be objective in the same way as scientific truth. Kitcher, I am suggesting, has not fully released himself from the scientific picture of moral progress that he exhorts us to reject.

That said, I should also add that I share Kitcher's skepticism about most forms of moral realism, and also his skepticism of the moral expertise of philosophers. But I think my reasons for skepticism are different from Kitcher's. His reasons are fundamentally, I think, based in his methodological naturalism: there is simply no room, ontologically speaking, for mind-independent moral truths in the picture of the world he accepts, which is the world as given to us by an ideal science. It follows that there are no people who are especially in touch with these objective truths. My own skepticism comes from a dislike of the idea that morality is something, like science, that can and should be theorized from a maximally neutral perspective—that to have moral understanding is just like having scientific understanding, except about moral matters rather than scientific matters. Indeed, my skepticism comes from a dislike of the idea that morality can be theorized at all: that moral truth is something that can be systematized, or even articulated discursively without loss or distortion.

What I have been trying to suggest is that we can have an account of moral discovery—or what I would prefer to call *moral seeing*—that does not implicitly harken to the scientific picture of discovery. On such an account, what's required to see the world aright, morally speaking, is to take up the correct morally loaded perspective. Taking up such a perspective is not a theoretical move, but a practical one, and it may even be that the content of such a perspective is not discursively available—cannot, that is, be articulated as a theory. The most faithful articulation of moral truth, then, will be found not in the theories of philosophers, but in the ethical practices of those at the forefront of moral progress: the moral and political revolutionaries, both known and unknown, both individuals and, importantly, groups, who call us into a better world. Such people will not generally be philosophers, or priests, or indeed people endowed with any recognized social authority. Indeed, they will be precisely the people that Kitcher identifies as the originators of moral progress, the people who first cry out against injustice: slaves, women, gays, workers.

2.

Leaving aside Kitcher's criticism of the Discovery View, I would like to turn to his positive account of moral progress. To simplify quite a bit, on Kitcher's view, moral progress occurs when there is a social change that (1) is a response to a situation that would be deemed problematic by relevant stakeholders deliberating together under ideal conditions, and (2) where that social change would be endorsed in an ideal conversation in which the perspectives of the relevant stakeholders were represented. So we have a picture of moral progress that consists in social changes that would be deemed by ideal collective deliberators to be good responses to genuine problems.

I think it is fair to say that the notion of ideal conversation and deliberation plays a very large role in Kitcher's account. Indeed, it is the *ideal* nature of the deliberation that is supposed to allow Kitcher to distinguish between genuine and nongenuine moral problems, and between legitimate and illegitimate resolutions to those problems, all without appealing to antecedent moral principles. Otherwise, Kitcher's account risks implying that, say, the complaints of white nationalists against immigrant populations constitute a genuine moral problem, one compromise solution to which might just be the expulsion (or worse) of people of color. To this prospect Kitcher will presumably want to say that an ideal conversation between relevant stakeholders—including the white nationalists and their nonwhite immigrants neighbors—will not yield the verdict that the plight of white nationalists is an urgent moral problem to be solved, or at least will not yield a resolution to that problem that involves harming the interests of nonwhite immigrants.

This raises the question of what it means for a conversation to be "ideal" in Kitcher's sense—and specifically, whether a morally neutral notion of idealness can do the work that Kitcher needs it to. When characterizing what makes a collective moral inquiry ideal, Kitcher talks about the importance of all stakeholders not only being represented but also sympathetically engaging with each other's perspectives and treating each other with deep mutual respect. But one might worry that if sympathy and engagement are going to do the work that Kitcher wants, they will have to be read as morally thick notions. For, when Kitcher says that the participants in an ideal conversation must "sympathize" with each other, he does not mean merely that they must be good at reading each other's minds. Psychopaths are extremely effective at knowing how other people feel and see the world; but, crucially, they do not care about how others feel or see the world. We could imagine white nationalists who were extraordinarily good at understanding just what it feels like to be a nonwhite immigrant, but being totally unmoved by this understanding. Similarly, when Kitcher says that the participants in an ideal conversation must respect each other, he presumably does not mean merely that they let others speak, that they listen to what other have to say, and so on. It is not enough for them to follow some pure formal procedures. He means, presumably, that they *see* each other as having equal moral weight, and so recognize that all proposed resolutions must be indifferent between their divergent interests. In other words, the participants in an ideal conversation must endorse and act on a principle of basic moral equality: they must recognize the moral worth of those with whom they deliberate. But then, again, we have a moral notion being built into our understanding of moral progress, via the putatively nonmoral notion of an "ideal" method of deliberation. If so, then Kitcher has not succeeded in giving us an account of moral progress that does not tacitly appeal to the notion of moral truth.

I do wonder, however, whether this really is Kitcher's project. A different way of understanding what Kitcher is up to is that he is offering us a practical methodology for collective moral decision-making, rather than a metaethical account of what moral progress consists in. If this is right, then the practical methodology might make reference to moral judgments about appropriate and inappropriate forms of sympathy, just as Rawls's original position involves deliberation among people with what Rawls calls a "sense of justice." On this second reading of Kitcher's project, his goal is not to offer us a new, naturalistic metaphysics of morals, but rather to offer us a practical, first-order procedure for going on as a moral community. On this second reading, Kitcher's project is not to advance a piece of moral metaphysics, but to offer us a piece of nonideal, first-order normative theory.

3.

How does Kitcher's proposal fare, so understood? For Kitcher, a close examination of moments of progressive historical change reveals approximations of his favored method of "democratic contractualism." He writes:

> Neglecting all the perturbations, we can trace the arc as it bends away from injustice. Initially, some brave individual, either a member of the marginalized class or someone with unusual sympathy for that class, speaks out loudly enough to force the attention of a small group among the privileged. The speakers are always vilified, and sometimes pay for their temerity with their lives. Their achievement consists in starting a public conversation. When it goes well, the conversation attracts more dissident voices and a wider circle of sympathetic listeners, so that later stages build on ground already conceded, shifts of opinion effected by earlier conversations.

On this picture, what has been crucial, historically, for moral progress has been collective conversation. This is not to say that Kitcher wholly ignores the role of violence, material struggle, or death in moral change: as he says, those who speak out against injustice often pay with their lives, and he identifies the protests of the marginalized as crucial for triggering moral conversations. But one might think that the history of much moral progress (again, such as it is) has not been fundamentally a history of conversation at all, but a history of power: the wielding of power by the dominant against the oppressed, and the eventual seizing of that power, or some small part of that power, by the dominated. Consider the fight for black civil rights in the United States or the Indian revolt against British rule. The moral progress of those moments was effected in part through new forms of speaking and listening and understanding. But it was also effected by the wrenching of power away from the white and colonial hegemony, often under the threat of violence. Similar things can be said about the end of American slavery, about the labor rights movement, about the feminist battle against patriarchy, and so on. In all these cases, change happened not (merely) because those in power became convinced that change should happen, but because their power to dictate the proper form of society was itself attacked and attenuated by the relatively powerless. In turn, the possibility of such shifts in power was in part created by underlying material changes—changes in patterns of economic production and social reproduction, new forms of civil unrest, independent political crises, foreign wars. Indeed, the genius of successful resistance movements lies not just in the conversations they wish to provoke, but in the creative repurposing of particular historical moments to their advantage.

None of this is to say that Kitcher's vision of democratic, egalitarian moral decision-making is not a worthy ideal. But seeing the history of moral progress through the lens of ideal conversation risks obscuring, I fear, a long history of resistance among the powerful toward such conversations—and with it, the various strategies that the relatively powerless have developed to force change in the absence of such conversations. Kitcher's model of moral progress also risks suggesting, falsely, that all marginalized people need to do today is *speak up*. In our highly non-Deweyan world, the ability for some people to speak, and to be truly heard, is an ability that itself presupposes a radical shift in power. And so while Kitcher might well be right that we would make swifter moral progress if we were capable of such idealized conversation, it is not clear that conversation itself will suffice to get us to that ideal.

Progress, Regress, and Power

Susan Neiman

Philip Kitcher's lectures on moral progress reveal the kind of philosophical sensibility his friends and admirers have come to expect
from him. Throughout his work, Philip displays a deep commitment to reasonableness and clarity, along with what I daresay is
wisdom: acknowledging, as he does throughout these lectures, the existence of human frailty, he nonetheless wants to spotlight those cases
where human beings have done what they should do in order to overcome that frailty itself. So I was excited to hear that he was planning
to discuss moral progress, for it's a topic on which I've often spoken,
though not in this detail or with this clarity. For that I'm regularly accused of naïve optimism. As much as I'd like to adopt Philip's account
in order to shore up the gaps in my own, much more inchoate one, I see
some real problems with it—all of them connected to the fact that not
everyone hears the sweet voice of reason as often as Philip does. The in-
cidence of moral deafness is getting higher all the time. The objections
I'll make are, of course, what commentators are meant to offer on such
occasions, but they are offered in the hope that Philip will refute them.
I would very much like to have an account of moral progress that's
more sure-footed, but I don't see how to get one on these terms. For
even if Philip takes pains to distinguish his view from what he calls
the Discovery View, I fear his approach is much too cognitive, relying
on a moral community of Philip (and Pat) Kitchers to examine moral
quandaries in good faith. Alas, it's not the Philip and Pat Kitchers of
the world—or the John Stuart Mills and Harriet Taylors—who present obstacles to moral progress. If a majority of agents were engaged
in sincere moral inquiry to begin with, the battle would be more than
half won.

Susan Neiman, *Progress, Regress, and Power* In: *Moral Progress.* Edited by: Jan-Christoph Heilinger,
Oxford University Press. © Oxford University Press 2021. DOI: 10.1093/oso/9780197549155.003.0006

Let me begin with some points of general agreement. I very much like his substitution of *progress from* for *progress to*. It solves ontological but more importantly practical problems of agreement on what, exactly, the goal of our exertions should be. (Hegel's vision of human history as a matter of progress toward greater freedom might command general agreement until you realize that he thought the Prussian state was an exemplar of it.) Similarly, Philip's approach solves the ontological problems of the Discovery View by denying there has to be an independent moral reality that somehow prescribes our conduct. Since I have an ontological problem that may just be a function of my lack of understanding, I want to mention it now. If, as Philip says, slavery was always wrong, whether or not it was recognized as such, what is it that the abolitionists discovered? I trust Philip can give me an answer to this, but it's not my main worry.

In fact, I think that, apart from philosophers, few people really have ontological problems. Even fundamentalists who believe that moral laws are given by an omnipotent Creator can get tripped up by the Euthyphro problem, and go on justifying their beliefs all the same. I don't mean to minimize the threat of fundamentalist forces, especially around issues of sex and gender, but let's face it: they aren't going to listen to us whatever we say. So my worries are not about those who want to put African Americans back on the plantations, women in the kitchens, and gays in the closet, but about another group entirely. Those who deny the reality of moral progress are not in doubt about what we should be progressing from, or even to. Indeed, the Left shows a remarkable degree of consensus and conviction on all those fronts. Their concerns are not about moral cognition, or recognition, but about power—specifically about the extraordinary power of the structures that be to co-opt progressive movements and to turn their achievements into losses or new forms of repression.

The criticisms I have in mind will be familiar. The battle to undo legal segregation in America seemed an unquestionable instance of moral progress, and I'd be hard-pressed to argue against it. Yet many have pointed out that the end of legal segregation led to the decline of strong, self-sustaining black communities by allowing access to wealth and opportunity to a talented tenth (Jay-Z just became rap music's first billionaire) and leaving behind substandard ghettos where black boys have a better chance of going to jail than of going to college.

The lessening of discrimination against women has led my daughters to take opportunities for granted that my generation had to struggle for and that my mother never imagined. Yet my daughters are not convinced that the outcome is progress. True, they are now expected to have a career rather than merely being permitted one. But they are also subject to a degree of sexual objectification that my generation never knew. #MeToo very much notwithstanding, they are expected to be competent professionals and look like porn stars at the same time. Philip's third case, gay rights, is a bit more complicated, but activists like Martin Duberman have argued that in gaining things like marriage equality, the gay rights movement lost the progressive edge that was its power.

I'm not endorsing all these criticisms, but I do worry about them. The problem, for such critics, is not that they're sincerely worried about knowing what is right, as in the kinds of cases of moral conflict that Philip detailed. They are quite certain—occasionally too certain perhaps—about what's right, but they're worried about what's possible in a world where every step forward seems to be undercut, as if by some fast-footed martial art, and transformed into a step in the wrong direction. It's the grandchildren of the *Dialectic of Enlightenment* generation, even for those who never read a word of Adorno or Horkheimer, and their concerns are deep enough to make resignation a problem— even for political acts as simple as voting. If every advance that you took as an instance of moral progress turns out to have regressive consequences no one could foresee at the time, isn't it better to sit on your hands?

Now, I happen to think the martial art that gently overthrows initial advances by co-opting them is called capitalism, and I suspect that Philip agrees with me. But to ask how we might make the moral progress that consists in undoing capitalism goes far beyond the scope of our discussion, so I want to raise the other problem I have with Philip's account, which I think is connected with the first. As Philip said in the second lecture, every instance of moral progress that he considers (and probably those he doesn't) contains a double movement: from factual ignorance to factual knowledge, and from contempt, disgust, and repulsion to sympathy and understanding. Moral progress thus has a cognitive and an emotional component. Philip is keen to stress, rightly on my view, that moral progress is less a matter of belief than of practice; moral truth, he says, is that which emerges when we make moral progress. My worry, however, is that the emotional component is much larger than Philip suggests, and that none of his additional dimensions nor any cognitive means are not enough to address it. Of course, he may mean to delve into these questions in the future, and I hope these remarks are helpful if he decides to fill out the noncognitive details.

Let's look again, briefly, at the abolition of slavery. Philip acknowledges, of course, that he's presented an idealized history, and that what happened involved "stuttering steps forward and lurches backward." Yet all the steps forward seem to turn on cognition, moral inquiry undertaken by individuals like John Woolman, who were startled out of moral deafness by a chance encounter that led them to "begin an unsystematic moral inquiry, seeking to learn about the conditions of life under slavery and the capacities of the slaves." I've no doubt this was the case for John Woolman, whose journal I have yet to read. But I think it assumes too much good faith on the part of the slaver traders to suggest that what they were lacking was information.

Now Cotton Mather's claim that slavery was needed to grant Africans eternal life under the Gospel is not incoherent with some conceptions of Christianity: after all, the Inquisition burnt white people to save their immortal souls, so why not enslave people in this lifetime if you can promise them a heaven in the next? Against this kind of logic, no new information can count. (The afterlife is notoriously, or conveniently, inaccessible.) But I'm more concerned about empirical knowledge. Philip says that nineteenth-century stereotypes about Africans began to crumble with more serious explorations of life in Africa. But the earliest European explorers of West Africa, the Portuguese, found flourishing kingdoms—many of which, alas, were willing to sell captured members of other tribes into slavery. Still they were hardly seen, or treated, as beastly savages; there are pictures from that time showing Europeans being received at African courts, so they knew there were complex social and legal structures; as for culture, some of the Benin bronzes date from the thirteenth century, long before Europeans arrived. In short, the picture of Africans as naked savages dancing around a fire, preferably with a human being roasting on it, is not the product of ignorance but of propaganda. The idea that Africans had culture wasn't something that had to be discovered; at best it was rediscovered and is still being rediscovered today. Nor do I think it was something that was simply overlooked. Maybe slave captains hadn't seen the Benin bronzes, but they knew enough about culture to make sure that slaves were regularly held, and shipped, with people from different tribes, so as to destroy the value of common language and, in time, those languages themselves. In response to this point, Philip has responded that while early slave traders had direct evidence of the richness of African cultures, by Cotton Mather's day, captured slaves were brought down to the sea, so there was no need for enslavers to travel to the interior; thus, they may have seen little of West African kingdoms and had no information to transport to New England. This may be true, but it would be interesting to research the question in depth. For whether or not Cotton Mather had any knowledge of those he considered savage, it's important to understand how that knowledge came to be suppressed. To understand how progress is made, understanding regress can be helpful.

If a change of knowledge wasn't a major factor leading to abolition, what about a change of empathy? I think how empathy toward African Americans grew, through narratives like Frederick Douglass's or novels like Harriet Beecher Stowe's, is less in need of explanation than the question of how empathy was so successfully suppressed. What was especially peculiar about the American South's peculiar institution was the nearness and complexity of slaveholder and slave. In some of the larger plantations of Mississippi and Louisiana, most slaves' lives were as remote from their owners as they were on the plantations of the Caribbean. But even in the latter, there were house slaves, and they were not only responsible for cooking and cleaning. They presided over the most intimate and vulnerable aspects of slaveholders' lives, accompanying birth and death and doing the lion's share of the child-raising. Northerners may have needed information in order to become abolitionists; though slavery existed in the North, it just wasn't as large or pervasive. But given the proximity between Southern slaveholders and their captives, it's hard to say that what changed was a matter of new information. (And, of course, in most cases, it did not change at all; abolition was regarded as a matter of victors' justice, and harsh forms of servitude, some even worse than slavery, continued in the South through the mid-twentieth century.)

So hear I'd like to hear more about the notion of false consciousness Philip has begun to develop, for I suspect it could help us understand how so many people could be so willfully blind and deaf to the truths that were there all around them, and that later generations find obvious. And it may help us to account for instances of moral regress—which in turn could shed light on moral progress itself. I don't want to begin a discussion of how in the world Barack Obama could be replaced by Donald Trump. But surely the racism that was a major part of whatever explanation we have was not fueled by an absence of knowledge. The whole world had just witnessed eight years of a president—and every member of his family!—who exemplified every quality you hope a national leader will have. It's my own suspicion that the resentment and hostility directed to the Obama family was rather a function of the fact that, taken together, they undermined every remaining racist cliché. But whether or not you agree with me, surely it's clear that eight years of Obama left no one who is capable of looking at evidence in doubt about African American abilities. (I am not joining what I've called the grandchildren of the *Dialectic of Enlightenment* generation in arguing that because Obama's election was followed by Trump's, the latter was not a true sign of progress. I am just asking about regress, and the role of cognition in it.)

As I was wondering about the ways a cognitive account of moral progress needs to be supplemented by an emotional account, I turned to reread Anthony Appiah's *The Honor Code*. Appiah looks at three cases of moral revolution—the abolition of dueling, the abolition of foot-binding, and the abolition of slavery—and argues that the facts about what were wrong with all those institutions were known long before the practices stopped. He cites tenth-century Chinese writers who deplored the fact that "Children not yet four or five years old, innocent and without crime, are caused to suffer limitless pain" when the bones of their feet were broken to satisfy a sexual fetish. So why did it take nearly a thousand years to move from a state in which Chinese parents (of the upper classes) could not find a husband for a daughter whose feet were unbound to the opposite? Within two generations, men refused to marry women whose feet had been bound. Appiah argues that in all these cases, what had been a mark of honor became a badge of dishonor or shame. It's a matter of creating the esteem in others' eyes Western philosophers know from Hegel.

I think Appiah is definitely on to something here. Of course, we need an account of how practices change from being honorable to seeming shameful, one he tries to fill with some deft historical narratives—when dueling, for example, once confined to gentlemen, reached the lower classes, it became less valued—literally declassed and ridiculous. Similar stories can be told about the way racism, even in the Deep South, became so embarrassing that every witness at the trial of those who murdered four girls in the 1963 Birmingham church bombing swore they'd never been against blacks or integration. This prompted the defense attorney to say that Martin Luther King's job would have been easier had he known my client was the only racist in Birmingham. But the trial was held in 2001; over a generation had passed, and those left from the previous generation knew that their children would be ashamed to acknowledge them, had they publicly stuck to their earlier convictions.

We could consider another case, closer to home. The generation of Germans who lived through the war was ashamed, at most, of having lost it. They considered themselves the war's greatest victims. It would take a generation, and a lot of work, before the majority of Germans felt shame about the crimes their nation had committed.

My only problem with Appiah's account is something he acknowledges himself: honor is itself in short supply these days. It plays a role within institutions, and not the least problematic of them: honor killings (as he acknowledges) take place in a number of traditional societies, gangs are particular about codes of honor, as is the military. While Appiah doesn't hold honor to be a moral property by itself, for all those reasons, he does think something has been lost in those liberal, progressive societies where it plays an increasingly small role. I wouldn't bet on a movement to restore honor codes. I do think that shame, and embarrassment, play a greater role in people's progress from unjust states to better ones, and I wonder if we could increase the enthusiasm for moral progress if we could figure out a way to make it cool or sexy. I know that the concept of cool is at least as vague as any other, and it certainly doesn't do all the work that Appiah's concept of honor does. At the München talks, Amia Srinivasan suggested that the concept "woke" would do the kind of work that I seek here. It's a helpful suggestion for thinking about ways in which the very concept of moral progress can be made not just more sure-footed but more alluring.

Progress as the Dynamics of Crisis

Rahel Jaeggi

Reviving the notion of progress is not an easy task today, nor is it a self-evident one. But it is of great importance. One of the concerns I decidedly share with Philip Kitcher is that we cannot do without a concept of progress and progressive social change in order to understand and evaluate our social life. His attempt to spell out a pragmatist, nonteleological conception of progress, as it is based on what I take to be his "materialist" concept of ethics, has the potential to refute the superficial critiques that the theories of social progress sometimes inspire. To comment on Philip Kitcher's project is therefore not only a great honor but also a special pleasure for me. It wouldn't be easy to find someone with whom I share as many intuitions as I do with him—and I have learned a lot from engaging with his work for some time now.

Let me start by spelling out my understanding of Philip's project and my general agreement with it, as based on his previous work, his discussion of the *Ethical Project*.[1] Based on the fact that we as human beings are in need of social cooperation and grapple with the attempt to stabilize this cooperation, the "Ethical Project" is the project of shaping and reshaping the modes of cooperation in question. Now, if we understand those attempts as modes of problem-solving, some of the changes that the institutions, practices, and understandings that constitute our communal and individual life undergo, are not only "mere changes" but can be conceived of as a "change for the better," that is, progressive social change.

---

[1] Philip Kitcher, *The Ethical Project* (Cambridge, MA: Harvard University Press, 2011).

Rahel Jaeggi, *Progress as the Dynamics of Crisis* In: *Moral Progress*. Edited by: Jan-Christoph Heilinger, Oxford University Press. © Oxford University Press 2021. DOI: 10.1093/oso/9780197549155.003.0007

As I understand it, this claim does not entail that our history so far has been a straightforward move toward the better; it need not even imply that we *experience* progress on the empirical level at all, even if Philip certainly thinks that it has taken place on some level and in some dimensions. What is implied is that we can *evaluate* certain practices and institutions as well as a certain way of organizing social cooperation and reproduction as a change for the better (or progress) in so far as problems have been solved. The idea of progress thus can serve (at least) as a normative criterion. But Philip wants more than that. Understanding how progress occurs should have, so Kitcher hopes, the practical impact of "making progress less contingent." To understand what we are doing enhances our abilities to intentionally pursue it. And to understand the obstacles to social progress might give us the means to do away with them (or so we hope).

Now, I am deeply sympathetic to the idea of progress as a problem-solving process including its underlying metaethical idea that progress precedes the "good," that is, the rejection of the "Discovery View." Most of all, I share Philip's conviction that we can and should develop a nonteleological notion of progress. Coming from fundamentally different philosophical backgrounds, we are in the same camp here. With so much agreement, where does the disagreement come in?

To put it boldly, what strikes me as problematic in Philip's approach is the slightly harmonistic and (in the end surprisingly) cognitivistic character of the process—as well as what I see as a neglect of the historical and the socio-structural dimension of the problems that provide the starting points for possible progress. What seems to get insufficient consideration are the power-driven structural and functional obstacles to progress as well as the moments of dysfunctionality and crisis so characteristic of problems that trigger the dynamics of social change. Moral progress, I contend, depends on a broader social context and thus is influenced by the manifold dynamics of social change; it is brought about (at any rate partly) by social struggles that react to more or less deeply seated structural contradictions and crises. Moral progress in terms of problem-solving, then, is not an innocent attempt to "get to know," to move from ignorance to knowledge, from a lack of empathy to moral sensitivity. It does not solely rely on the capacity to take over the other's perspective and to enter an ideal and open-minded conversation.

1. The Problem with Problems

How, then, do moral improvements come about? How is it that social practices and institutions like slavery, discrimination of homosexuals, and the domination of women (to use Philip's well-established examples) which were perceived as normal and morally unobjectionable for centuries become an object of public opprobrium and are increasingly abandoned? What kinds of changes are involved and what triggers them?

Moral progress, I agree, is problem-solving. Moral progress (and progress in general) is triggered by problems. Problems come up as a disturbance of our social order and moral infrastructure. Progress, however, is what solves these problems. But I do think that our respective takes on what a problem is differ.

The Problem as Crisis

Now, as Philip is very much aware, putting the existence of "problems" at center stage raises obvious questions: How do we even know that we have a problem? Who decides what counts as a problem? Given that institutions like slavery, the domination of women, and the exclusion of homosexuals existed for centuries and were taken for granted by the mainstream of society—without ever having been conceived of as a problem—this is not a trivial question. Obviously, identifying problems in the realm of the social is not as easy as discovering engine damage on a broken car. The existence and identification of problems will be as disputed as their respective solutions. Some people don't even see the slightest sign of a problem where others perceive a dramatic and damaging crisis.

The first difficulty here is the *epistemic status of problems*. Problems are not brute facts. They depend on interpretations and the reaction of the people involved. Yet, at the same time, if they are to point to a genuine progress narrative, they have to be more than subjective sensations and constructs. Whether we confront a problem or not cannot be up to us.

Philip's solution to this challenge is what can be called a *qualified subjectivism*. Departing from Berkeley's suggestion that "a situation is problematic if those who find themselves in it seek relief from it," he suggests that we modify and qualify the criteria under which "seeking relief" is adequate. "Situations are problematic when they are rightly judged problematic." Thus, instead of simply "appealing to *actual* feelings" (which would lead to a strong and unqualified subjectivism), Philip suggests that we pay attention to *justified* feelings. Justification, then, is what emerges out of a conversation in which all who are concerned would be heard and considered on equal terms and (another qualification) don't suffer from false consciousness. This is a quite sophisticated version of what has been called "preference laundering" in order to arrive at sound criteria for what people "really" want, for their qualified wishes and desires.

Still, I wonder whether starting with subjective feelings in the first place does not lead us away from a genuinely pragmatist focus on problems (and from what the reference to problems can do for our understanding of progress.) Problems, as I see them, have an objective side and a practical impact. In a pragmatist spirit: if we have a problem, things don't work out smoothly, and we then experience hindrances in the course of affairs that we usually take for granted. There is a moment of *dysfunction* and *crisis* inherent in the concept of a problem that should not be forgotten. Whether it is adequate to bring something up as a problem, then, depends on whether it addresses a "real" dysfunction or crisis, something that happens in the world and not in our reaction to it alone. John Dewey's approach to problems is masterful insofar as he moves back and forth between the objective and the subjective side, between realism and constructivism toward problems. He recognizes, on the one hand, that a problem must always first be comprehended and conceptualized as such in order to become a problem. The problem does not exist unless it is perceived as a problem; that is, it does not exist without the process of inquiry that detects it and makes it tangible as such.

Therefore, problems are something we construct. We do not find them somewhere, but make them.[2]

On the other hand, Dewey insists on the objective character of problems, that they arise out of reality. We do not raise the problems ourselves. Problems arise. We do not invent the problems, but react to them. From this perspective, problems cannot be dismissed without consequences, and one cannot pose them arbitrarily either. Thus, the problem lies on the side of reality, not with us. It's the situation that is problematic. As Dewey holds, we can't make up problems (in the end); neither can we deny them (in the long run.) A problem, then, is at the same time *given* and *made*. It is *made* insofar as the problem first has to be extracted from initially indeterminate material; it is *given* insofar as a situation exhibits signs of a crisis.

So instead of the qualified subjectivism that Kitcher seems to defend, I would, following Dewey, suggest a *qualified objectivism*, an approach that can make sense of the moment of dysfunction. My view is the following: *problems* (as we are interested in them here) are not just instances of recognized or unrecognized *suffering* and disagreement that are in the way of an ideal conversation and the respective social arrangements. They should be seen as moments of *crisis and dysfunction* with an objective side, leading to obstacles and hindrances within the course of affairs of our practical social life. It is this crisis and the moment of dysfunction that gets the "moral conversation" started in the first place. (And it's the crises or the obstacles, hindrances, or contradictions in the course of affairs and the self-understanding of a community that serves as a criterion, a truth-maker in the contentious process of bringing a problem on the agenda.)

Now, one might say: slaveholding society worked out quite well for the slaveholders; it was perfectly functional as a society. The same might be the case with respect to misogyny and homophobia. It is only from the perspective of the dominated, oppressed, and excluded that the situation was and increasingly became problematic. But then, from the perspective of social progress, one would have to claim that the fact that one group is oppressed and excluded itself poses a problem for

[2] For a discussion of problems and the idea of solving problems of a second order see my *Critique of Forms of Life* (Cambridge, MA: Harvard University Press, 2018).

society as a whole—it leads to modes of social cooperation that can't be stable in the long run. Without this kind of "normative functionalism" at place—that is, roughly, the idea that what is at stake with progress as a problem-solving process is not only justice or morality alone but normative aspects that are deeply intertwined with functional ones— addressing the situation as "problematic" might not be adequate at all. It would then be a conflictual situation and what happened when slavery was finally abolished was not the solution of a *problem* but the winning of a *conflict*. That the winning of a conflict (without reference to a problem solved) would probably not even count as progress brings to the fore that the notion of "progress" addresses issues that have some overarching significance. The perspective that we buy into with the idea of progress and the idea of progress as problem-solving is a comprehensive view. It is not only about one side being better off now but about (in broad terms) society being better of as a result of this side being better off, that is, as a result of diminishing sources for conflicts and tensions.

So, if we, as I suggest, hold on to the idea of progress and problemsolving, and if we don't just want to claim that to own slaves and dominate women is morally wrong (which they certainly are—but this is not the point of applying the concept of *progress* and does not exhaust its explanatory as well as normative potential), we have to insist that the slaveholder society as well as the patriarchal society had problems in terms of dysfunctions, dissonances, and inner contradictions. I cannot pursue this here in detail, but let me mention that Joshua Cohen in his famous essay "The Arc of the Moral Universe" tried to make the case for exactly this thesis (while arguing that chattel slavery eroded or collapsed because it was morally objectionable).[3] A problem in this (objective) sense takes on the character of a crisis, even if we still admit that a problem has to be interpreted and conceived of as a problem in order to count as one, and even if we insist that a crisis that does not at some point turn into a conflict (and doesn't show up on the level of individual's suffering) might not be one.

---

[3] Joshua Cohen, "The Arc of the Moral Universe," *Philosophy & Public Affairs* 26, no. 2 (1997): 91–134.

Now, what happens to Philip's Victorian couple at the fireplace if we think of it in terms of crisis and social dysfunction? We introduce another perspective. Remember the vast array of literature that depicts this age, this form of life, as driven by denial and unresolved and latent crises in all stages and dimensions. Analyzing the situation of the well-meaning husband, we will then not only find false consciousness and mauvaise foi on the level of the individuals but a pathological marriage due to a pathological social environment, a marriage in which, whatever else happens and whatever coping mechanisms are in place, something is wrong. The unequal standing of the partners, as we might sketch it out, undermines the idea of love that at the same time informs the social narrative of marriage—and this "inner contradiction" leads to an uneasy and crisis-prone situation. We might expect that those features lead to a social situation that actually "does not work" in some important respect, crying out for all sorts of compensation in order to reach a balance that is prone to be unstable. Those contradictions and tensions cause inadequate reactions and will formation; thus, to detect false consciousness depends on an analysis of the underlying tensions.

How does this approach differ from what is captured by (an aggregate of) subjective experiences of suffering? Perhaps the differences are inconspicuous at first glance. In the end, *qualified objectivism* takes the subjective side into account, whereas a *qualified subjectivism* finds its way to the objectivity of the problem through investigating deformations in the formation of the will. Don't they end up in a similar position then? The two approaches work on a different level. Instead of starting with the individual's feelings, the "objective" or crisis-related approach starts from an analysis of the tension within social formations, the situation to which the individual reacts. In part, this is a question of which approach has the better prospect of solving the notoriously difficult task of coming up with a criterion for "false consciousness." False consciousness is, in a first approximation, false since it is an inadequate reaction to a problematic situation. The objective crisis or situation then turns out to be a standard against which to judge, as in Dewey's concept of a problem, the kind of phenomenon that you can't ignore because it meets us with resistance.

Problems, Conflict, and Power

While I have emphasized so far the crisis side, the dysfunctional character of problems, and discussed the epistemic issue of identifying problems, there is yet another aspect to take into account, the conflictual and possibly agonistic nature of problems.

I have already mentioned it in passing: Who is the "we" that has a problem? The problem of one group might be the advantage of the other (as is the case with slavery as well as with the patriarchal and heteronormative gender regime). This then would be a deep-seated conflict, which brings me to a feature that worries me in the portrayal of moral progress that Philip has provided us with: its slightly asymmetric and harmonistic tendency (a problem that he might easily solve but that also might lead to deeper issues).[4]

What we don't get to see is how interests, power structures, deep social structures of exploitation and domination are effective in sustaining a situation that—from a moral point of view—is defective. The ideal conversation that would lead to moral progress (that would be the methodological path to moral progress) is not only obstructed by epistemic errors, failures of empathy, and false consciousness, but by *deep-seated social structures of domination*. What prevents moral progress is not only a lack of knowledge and affection and bad habits such as implicit bias and stereotyping. While it certainly makes sense to spell out how those work, what analysis should be doing here is understanding how those problems (racism, sexism) are functional for sustaining a certain social order.

This reveals a danger that goes along with all kinds of problem-solving accounts (my own included). If the problem-solving account seems to imply that problems in need of a solution are problems

---

[4] When he talks about overcoming the moral deafness and avoiding exclusions, when he depicts how slaveholders and the general public have come to see slavery as scandalous and evil, the agency of those who are enslaved and dominated certainly plays some role in terms of their heroism and the sacrifices. Still, inclusion and the ideal conversation seems to be something that is primarily and one-sidedly granted by those who already are in power—who have the power to set the agenda and to include others who then will become part of the club. But the game-changing role of social movements sometimes leads to a change of rules as such (and thus to transforming the club instead of its extension or boundaries).

for all, one should not forget that some people *benefit* from a racist, sexist, or inegalitarian social order, while others do not. To think of certain professions and occupation as "inadequate" for women is not just a failure of insight, something "we" could know better. To exclude women from public occupations, to condemn them to providing the "shadow work" of (unpaid, unrecognized) social reproduction and to provide the men, who are in power, with a "haven in a heartless world" is a way of organizing the social division of labor unfairly. The obstacles to moral progress and the problems we have to overcome, then, are not so much deficits in moral awareness but deep-seated social structures, effects of power and domination.

One more time the path for moral progress does not lead "from ignorance to knowledge" alone, it is a conflictual dynamics of social change in which the social division of labor, structured by domination has to be reorganized. The human form of cooperation is then not only endangered by "altruism failure" (as Kitcher develops in his eminent "Ethical Project") but also very often in the course of human history structured by domination. This, then, is not only a difference with re-spect to the *intensity of social change* (do we just talk and persuade each other or do we have to fight and overthrow the social order, if necessary also by employing violence?) but the insight that we have to face a *real conflict*, deeply seated in the institutions and practices of our societies.

To be clear: I don't suggest abandoning the notion of problem and replacing it by "conflict," which would imply giving up on the over-arching perspective. But it would then be that the problem of a society is its markedness by conflicts such as the ones mentioned.

Detecting moments of false consciousness, "giving a voice to those who suffer but don't cry," then, is one task for philosophy. Investigating the social functions of those (ethically deplorable) institutions and practices that are involved is another. To come up with a slogan (and shortcut) here: it is not about false consciousness alone but about what in the Marxist tradition is called "*necessary* false consciousness": nec-essary not so much because it would be inevitable but because its false-ness is the—adequate—reflection of a false reality. The problem here is not on the side of the individuals (even if individuals and groups of individuals are needed to overcome it) but on the side of the so-cial structure. A typology of blockages to (moral) progress is needed, then, that includes but is not exhausted by the inability to take over perspectives and also includes systematic impediments to collective action, ideologies, and socially induced "hermeneutical lacunas" (Miranda Fricker). In order to detect those dysfunctions, one needs a "deeper" analysis of a social structure and its functional necessities.

This leads to another issue. Is it actually an aggregate of individuals, the sum of all individuals concerned and their respective moral shortcomings and insensitivities, that has to be overcome in order to achieve progress? Do societies make moral progress, or is it the individual (eventually aggregated to collectives) that does so? We touch here on a foundational level of social theory or even social ontology. Philip's perspective seems to have an individualistic or atomistic bias (no matter that we both are talking about collectives), whereas I would suggest localizing progress on the level of "individuals-in-relation," on the level of forms of life or "Sittlichkeit" (ethical life). Social problems or dysfunctions, then, are not accumulations of individual ones. Neither is moral progress an accumulation of individual achievements alone but something that not only affects the moral community but can only be brought about within a moral community and through a change of its practices and institutions on a structural level.[5]

2. Moral Progress and Social Change

How, then, do we get from here to there? And why (even in the cases Philip focuses on) did it take us so long to get there?

[5] To move away from methodological individualism means to see the constitutive role that our embeddedness in social practices, relations, institutions has for our self-understanding and for what we are as persons—that is, an ontological primacy of the social (not to be confused with one in terms of a normative priority). Our communal life then is not just something that we value, that we cherish, that is part of our living a good life; it is not a good that we might have to balance with other goods. We can't make sense of ourselves unless we conceive of ourselves within these relations, involved in practices and institutions that shape and give content to who we are. So if Dewey (in "Individualism, Old and New" [New York: Minton, 1930]) says: "What one is as a person is what one is as associated with others, in a free give and take of intercourse," this is not a statement merely about the empirical importance of community but an attempt to criticize a misunderstanding, a misconceived self-conception: the individualistic misunderstanding, and the tensions and contradictions that, as a result, mark our institutions.

To identify social processes in which moral progress happens, to be able to describe how we get from *here* (a misogynist and homophobe society or a slaveholder society) to *there* (to emancipation and inclusion) is a crucial point in Kitcher's approach. And rightfully so. The genesis of social change has some impact on its validity for those who depart from what Philip has called the Discovery View. So I will try to elaborate a bit further in which respects I differ from his evolutionary account of moral progress in order to figure out some of our differences.

My thesis is this: what changes when moral progress occurs is not only our *moral* convictions and respective practices but a whole ensemble of practices, a form of life. Moral progress, I want to claim, can be understood only in the context of a more comprehensive dynamic of social change. It is *change within change*. In order to understand moral progress, we thus have to somehow change our focus. We should not isolate moral progress from the practical contexts and institutions in which it evolves. It has to be seen in the context of a plurality of dynamics that interact with each other. All of those are solving problems—but not all of those problems are moral problems.

Moral progress, as a result, *does not stand on its own*. It is framed by *social context and background conditions* and is reliant on them, even if moral *virtuosi* exist whose judgment is ahead of their time and social context.[6] Therefore, the change in the normative evaluation of institutions *and* in their practically effective form described as "moral progress" would not be the result of independent moral insight or of an independent development of the faculty of moral empathy, as Philip sometimes seems to suggest. It would instead be the effect of a change of whole social formations, of a change in the *surrounding or adjacent practices* and of the social horizon of interpretation within which the moral practices in question can be understood and stabilized. If we ask why certain practices and institutions that are outrageous or even unthinkable and unintelligible to us today could have been conceived of

---

[6] See for this my essay: "Resistance to the Perpetual Danger of Relapse: Moral Progress and Social Change," in Amy Allen and Eduardo Mendieta, *From Alienation to Forms of Life: The Critical Theory of Rahel Jaeggi* (University Park, PA: Penn State University Press, 2017).

as totally normal and acceptable, the answer is: They were normal in the context of those surrounding practices. The "plausibility" of what we at some point might judge as morally unacceptable depends on its social context, the fact that it is embedded in an ensemble of other practices and institutions that fit together and "normalize" it. This has an impact on Philip's question. Why did it take us so long to realize the outrageousness and brutality of homophobia, sexism, and slavery? Because they were (and in some respect still are) integrated in the normal course of our ethical life and the "problems" that came with the social arrangement in question either did not become as obvious or as urgent—or the opportunity for opening up the respective social arrangement did not arise.

This becomes apparent when we investigate the example of "marital rape" and domestic violence (as one of the rather shocking manifestations of gender domination).

The de facto toleration of marital rape (in Germany until 1997, rape was defined by law as an "extramarital occurrence") was situated in the context of other provisions of marriage law—for example, the bizarre state of affairs (again, in West Germany) that a husband could dissolve his wife's employment contract at will and also could dispose freely over his wife's property, provisions that remained in effect until 1953. It is situated in the context of a social arrangement in which women are typically economically dependent on their husbands and fits with the interpretation of marriage as an intimate community of fate and an "organic unity" that would be disrupted by the interference of law. From the general "duty of obedience" of the wife operative here, it seems to be but a small step to the duty of sexual obedience. A specific interpretation of male and female sexuality may also have contributed to the fact that a violent violation of the woman's sexual integrity could even be conceived as a variety of *sexual relations*, and not instead under the aspect of *violence*—as we nowadays say "sexualized violence" (with an emphasis on violence). Similar embedding relationships could be demonstrated for slavery and homophobia.

The formation of our moral perception, then, is not merely a change in our "moral sense" or "moral awareness," and not only a result of engaging in a moral conversation. Instead, it can be attributed to change in the background conditions, the subsequent practices and interpretations, which transforms the surroundings of the morally relevant practice in such a way that they appear in a different light.

How then do changes come about? If different practices are interconnected in the ways described, then the changes they undergo can be explained in terms of shifts in a nexus of practices—shifts which are caused by the dissolution of the relevant "relations of fit" and can be traced back to tensions (or even contradictions) between coexisting practices and their interpretations.

In such situations, relations of fit have become eroded and correspondingly vulnerable. New practices (and new technologies) are added to an ensemble of practices and interpretations; the conditions under which the latter are exercised, as well as their interpretation, undergo change. Some practices *fit* into the ensemble, whereas others seem to break it apart—so that in some cases an entire nexus of social practices undergoes a complete or partial shift. It is when a whole constellation changes that a specific moral institution can become peculiar, weird, repugnant, or outlandish and can then be thematized, rejected, and denounced by social actors or social movements.

A well-documented example of this is the social shifts in gender relations that occurred during and after World War II as a consequence of women entering into work relations that had previously been closed to them and assuming sole responsibility for the upkeep of the family. But inconspicuous technical inventions can also "trigger" social and moral changes. What makes the television series *Downton Abbey* so ingenious is its depiction of how love, war, radio, the telephone, and the typewriter combined with the ineffectiveness of aristocratic agriculture generate an irresistible dynamic of transformation that undermined—and would ultimately destroy—the way of life of the English aristocracy.

While Kitcher emphasizes how rocky and full of disturbances the transition called moral progress is, my picture is even messier since it is sometimes a result of a complex concatenation of intended and *unintended consequences of action* that brings about progress. *Changes in one complex of practices*—the invention of the typewriter, the invention of the pill, or the invention of gunpowder—can give rise to *changes in another area*, without, sometimes, anyone actively intending the changes in question.

I am not sure how much this narrative about moral change differs from Philip's, and maybe it is only a friendly amendment. But I do think that my approach takes the idea of problem-solving in a somewhat different direction in some respects.

(1) First of all, assuming that *moral progress* (as described) *unfolds within the broader context of social change*, hence in situations in which, together with the established moral judgments and institutions, other ethical, technical, and cultural practices also undergo change or become "obsolete," change is not brought about by a moral conversation alone but by an encompassing practical transformation of the practices and modes of cooperation that make up our social life. It develops in a nonendogenous way. We can call this a "materialist" dimension without arguing for a one-sided determinism. We are confronted here with a multiplicity of dynamics, not with a single one. Proceeding from a web of different practices *each* with its own logic of problem-solving, its own specific normative character, and the resulting dynamic, moral progress is not one-sidedly dependent on or determined by the other changes, thus not completely exogenous either. We have to understand, then, how these dynamics, the somewhat "messy" tangle of ideas, practical changes, and their interpretive "recuperation" are interconnected and influence each other. It is a social theory that is required here.

(2) Arguing against the tendency to isolate moral progress leads us to fundamentally change our understanding of moral progress in yet another respect. By embedding moral attitudes and practices in a more comprehensive context of practices, they are placed in a continuum with other dimensions of social practice, together with their respective forms of knowledge. As a result, it becomes possible to regard them as something that plays a role in the practical life of society and contributes to coping with its "life problems." At this point I want to push Philip further in what I conceive of as a pragmatist direction and bring it in tune with what I see as his own functionalist approach to morality. If the "Ethical Project" is about social cooperation, the modes of cooperation and their interpretation change with the (material)

circumstances under which they are performed. Organizing social cooperation, we are faced with a continuum of practical questions: instrumental ones as well as ethical and moral ones. And they are not independent from each other.

But this also obscures the distinction between ethics and morality that Philip defends. This is obviously a long conversation in ethics and moral philosophy that can't be solved here. But I don't see how social cooperation on any level can develop without ethics in the broad sense of a normative guidance on how to live our life, the normative patterns that constitute our social practices and (therefore) our social life. Even if some of it is led by prereflective habits, even if interpretations and attempts to make sense of the situation are not always in the open: Ethics is not restricted to the luxury question "What kind of person do I want to be?" but engrained in the everyday practices of every human group able to cooperate—and as such prior to morality, if we want to go for this as a categorical distinction at all.

(3) My narrative would also provide us with a slightly different answer to Philip's question of why it took us so long. Social transformations (and the respective moral progress), according to my account, do not arise out of nothing. They are motivated by problems and crises such that existing practices and institutions "no longer function" or confront a problem they cannot solve. Social (and moral) change becomes possible where there is a mismatch between different social practices and institutions, thus where the relation of fit between them is no longer exact. It becomes necessary when the erosion of social institutions and practices calls for the formation of new institutions. So, why has moral progress not happened earlier? Why did not already Oscar Wilde's attempt in changing the situation succeed, and why had generations of LGBTQs to suffer from social exclusion and medical treatments before the first liberal reforms could be celebrated, so Philip asks. Ruling out that this is just a contingent matter, his answer seems to be: Because we didn't apply the correct method. We didn't include all affected. But we could have arrived at the right method anytime; applying the

correct method would have been possible throughout history. My answer, however, is historicized: It took us so long because the "time was not ripe" or had not yet come. In my terms, the adjacent practices and enabling conditions were not yet there. This is not to argue for some kind of historical determinism or automatism. Nor do I want to speak for quietism. But I do want to argue for a view that takes history into account as a constellation that needs to be in place before the "world-historical individual" (Hegel) or a world-historical social movement can do its work.

What does this tell us about the possibility of making progress "less chancy"? If the possibility of change, the possibility of turning moral wrong into an object of opprobrium (as feminists did in the case of rape and revolting slaves and abolitionists in that of slavery), is bound up with shifts and with disjointed relations of fit in various fields, as I have argued, it is both correct and a simplification to say that social change rests on "social struggles" or social movements and on social actors willing to take risks (as Philip has it). Neither the existence nor the success of those progressive endeavors rests exclusively on the will and resoluteness of the actors involved. Neither does it rest on pure luck (even if there is some involved). These will depend rather on social and material enabling conditions that must be fulfilled if social actors are to be able to make practical interventions. Against a "voluntaristic" interpretation, social change (following Marx) calls as much for a passive as for an active element.

(4) But this has consequences for another crucial issue: The relation between *progress and history* and the evaluation of social change as change for the better. Concepts of progress, so it has been said, should be able to distinguish *mere change* from *change for the better*.

Now, progress, according to Philip's nonteleological approach is not "progress to" an already established normative goal, but "progress from" the problems that bother us. We work ourselves through practical problems without having established a definite end. One sees how this departs from a *teleological view*. Equal consideration, inclusion, or democracy (in a Deweyan society that "gives the oppressed a steady voice") is not a reified goal, not something we aim at and might gain as a trophy at the end of our journey but a mode of operation, a process.

If I understand Philip's program correctly, there is no way to come up with standards for moral progress by referring to the *content* of the change in question. It is the *method* that does the job. In an interesting way, then, the method employed is not only a tool for bringing about progress; it also provides us with the criterion for judging whether a certain transformation can be seen as change for the better. In the end, so it turns out, it is the application of the right or adequate method for solving problems in living together that settles whether a feature of social change is progressive or not: only those problems are good candidates for progressive change that are qualified as such by an inclusive (and rational) community. Progress is an open-ended learning process toward the realization of such a community. Only those problem-solutions, then, are progressive that have been arrived at by the right method—that is, by an inclusive and democratic (in Dewey's wide sense) conversation. Philip's is, thus, a *procedural approach*.

But then a question arises. How does this differ from other well-known procedural approaches like the one Habermas defends in his discourse ethics? Or, to put it differently: how does it differ from *deontological* approaches, from procedural approaches based on deontology? This is important for the normative question at stake. Deontological-procedural views have famously been accused of hiding their already established normative commitments in the procedure. The outcome of the procedure would then be the norms that have always been there, waiting for us to discover and to realize them. This is not what Philip can go for, since he wants to establish an alternative to the discovery view. The difference seems to be that he does not transcendentalize the procedure in question. His is supposed to be a real, not a counterfactual learning process. "Democracy" does not evaporate into ideal speech conditions; the community seems to be a real, not an idealized, moral community.

But, then, if we don't work with pre-established norms that guide us, how can we tell apart changes from changes for the better? Deontologists at this point claim that some normative principle (an idea about what we owe to each other) is needed as a guiding principle. But since Philip defends the "priority of progress," that is, the good is the result of the problem-solving process that we call progress, do we then not need to spell out the problem-solving process as a genuine process of learning? We might then need a *cumulative account of problem-solving*, a learning process that is cumulative in a qualitative sense and comes up to what Dewey called "growth" in order to solve the normative challenge. It is at this point that history comes in again, the kind of normative history that has informed so many theories of progress (like Hegel's) in the past. The historical dynamics of social crises, conflicts, and contradictions leads to an ongoing attempt to solve these problems: to adjust to the "new" and reintegrate the situation but also to accumulate experiences, to "learn" from whatever has come up as a crisis and, as a result, establish new ways of coping and new normative demands. It is this dimension of a cumulative history that seems to be missing in Philip's approach.

Now, the idea of accumulation or growth (not to be confused with falling back into teleology) is certainly not easy to defend, since it relies on an idea of how problems and their solutions somehow connect at least over the course of some part of history—an account of the erosion and transformation of social practices and institutions that is not completely contingent but based on the assumption of some social rationality of problem solving. But I'm not sure whether we can solve the normative problem without some reference to a learning process of this kind.

RESPONSE

Response to the Commentaries

Philip Kitcher

I

When I learned that Rahel, Susan, and Amia had agreed to comment on my lectures, I was delighted. I expected that they would provide excellent commentaries. But when I heard their actual remarks . . . I was even more delighted. My advance confidence had been more than justified. I am most grateful to them for their careful listening and reading, for their thoughtful—and challenging—questions, doubts and suggestions, and for the wonderfully constructive tone that permeates their reactions to my project. Philosophical discussion has come a long way since Janice Moulton taught the American philosophical community about the deficiencies of treating our subject as a combat sport. Amia, Susan, and Rahel are models for further progress.

Each of the commentaries offers some distinctive points, but there is one issue on which they converge. All three are concerned that I neglect asymmetries in power, and that I ignore the positive role played by seizures of political power. Any line of objection elaborated independently by three astute thinkers deserves a careful and extensive reply. So I shall begin, in the next three sections, by taking up the questions voiced individually by Amia, Susan, and Rahel. The final section will turn to the worry they all share.

II

Srinivasan starts with my disagreement with the Discovery View, and with my metaethics. She sees me as attempting to contrast moral progress with scientific progress, but, ultimately, as failing to liberate

Philip Kitcher, *Response to the Commentaries* In: *Moral Progress*. Edited by: Jan-Christoph Heilinger,
Oxford University Press. © Oxford University Press 2021. DOI: 10.1093/oso/9780197549155.003.0008

myself fully from a "scientific picture of moral progress." Many delicate questions are entangled here. Since my lectures didn't tease them apart, Srinivasan's worries are eminently reasonable. I appreciate the opportunity to offer a more extensive (and nuanced) account.

Insofar as moral philosophers think about moral progress, the vast majority of them adopt the Discovery View. That view comes in two species, a realist version committed to identifying moral progress with the acquisition of moral truth, and a noncognitivist version, according to which moral progress consists in acquiring improved sentiments. Derek Parfit, Thomas Nagel, and T. M. Scanlon figure as my paradigm realists; Allan Gibbard represents noncognitivism. Now, *given a certain picture of science*, it's correct to conclude that the Discovery View assimilates moral progress to scientific progress, and that I am opposing this assimilation. *If* adherents of the Discovery View accept the picture, then my disagreement with them can be posed as my rejection of a *common view* of scientific progress as a model for moral progress.

Since I reject the common view, I'd prefer not to set up the issue in those terms. Like Thomas Kuhn and Larry Laudan, I take scientific progress to be nonteleological. Scientific progress is driven from behind, as investigators attempt to resolve the significant problems of their current practices—hence, in some respects, I continue the practice of viewing moral progress as akin to scientific progress, thus becoming more deeply guilty of Srinivasan's charge! My general pragmatist project is committed to rethinking issues of progress, truth, objectivity, and knowledge across the board. Moreover, in thinking about kinship between science and morality, it's crucial to differentiate the respects in which the enterprises are said to be alike. Similarity with respect to objectivity need not betoken similarity in method—and conversely. As I'll try to show, some of Srinivasan's concerns rest on conflating distinctions of this kind.

At the heart of her metaethical critique is a penetrating question about the ontological presuppositions of historical explanation. With respect to factual discoveries, I claimed, historical explanations work because we understand how the activities of the discoverers put them in a position to recognize new entities. Perhaps foolishly, I appealed to a relatively complicated scientific case. I might have done better to begin with an everyday example of geographical discovery.

Which European first discovered North America? Apparently it was not Christopher Columbus, but the Icelander Leif Erikson (or possibly an even earlier Viking explorer). Any adequate narrative of the discovery will refer to Erikson's voyage to "Vinland" (or possibly to the journey of the supposed predecessor). A rival historical account, attributing the discovery to the sedentary Sven Swenson, who, the sources maintain, never stirred more than a mile from his Icelandic hamlet, would be less than fully convincing. Discovering a distant place requires, minimally, going to a location from which you can observe or detect it.

Lavoisier is often credited with the discovery of oxygen—and he surely gave us the name—but he was by no means the first to isolate the gas. His friend, correspondent, and scientific rival, Joseph Priestley, produced samples, and his reports taught Lavoisier how to do the same. Others prior to Priestley may also have separated more-or-less pure oxygen, but they seem to have been unaware that they had isolated a distinctive gas, differentiating them from Priestley, who called it "dephlogisticated air." Yet, however, the credit is to be assigned, it's highly unlikely to go to the favorite candidate of a revisionist historian, who attributes it to some early human predecessor, someone who made the discovery in simply inhaling.

Discoveries occur when a process of the "appropriate" kind generates in the discoverer some "suitable" psychological state. The difficulties of the concept of discovery emerge in specifying the conditions on appropriateness and suitability. Even without a full account, as with obscenity, we know it when we see it, and, importantly, we know it when we don't see it. Successful historical explanations of factual discoveries present to us processes that are recognizably appropriate and that issue in psychological outcomes that are recognizably suitable.

Sometimes, though, anthropologists and historians tell us about people who *thought of themselves* as making discoveries by acting in a particular way. Ethnologists describe how informants contact the spirits of the dead by chewing a root or smoking a weed. Medieval historians report on procedures for detecting witches, by dunking them, for example. Typically, readers don't endorse the verdicts of the communities under study. The processes engaged in are viewed as inappropriate. You can't reach out to the dead or identify women who have had commerce with the devil by doing those sorts of things—any more than stay-at-home Sven Swenson can discover a distant continent.

Where do the proposals of moral realists fit among the examples of successful and unsuccessful claims about discovery? There's an important difference between the approach favored by Parfit and that adopted by Nagel and Scanlon. Parfit feels no need to specify the character of the processes through which moral truths are apprehended or to characterize the moral reality thereby discovered. His realism is defended by analogy with mathematics, a case, he supposes, in which we're confident of the existence of an underlying mathematical reality and of our ability to detect its fundamental properties, without being able to say much either about the ontology or the epistemology. To my mind, exactly the same arguments apply in the mathematical and moral cases, and mathematical realism (like moral realism) should be discarded. Indeed, comparing the ways in which historians write about mathematical discoveries and their treatment of other sorts of cognitive advances inspires a serious account of the growth of mathematical knowledge.[1]

By contrast, Nagel and Scanlon suppose that there are objective truths about what people have reason to do, and they take moral discoveries to consist in further identifications of these reasons. I used the case of John Woolman to motivate a skeptical stance with respect to the Nagel-Scanlon approach. Without being told something about how people discriminate genuine reasons from pretenders to that title, it's impossible to differentiate Woolman's achievement from the missteps of the defenders of slavery with whom he debated the issue. What exactly did Woolman do that counts as coming to recognize reasons? A historical account, indeed Woolman's own journal, can tell us how he came to oppose slaveholding. How would Nagel or Scanlon pinpoint the crucial process(es) that generated a discovery of the reasons underlying his opposition? Why, given their (imprecise) account of what Woolman is supposed to have discovered, should we

---

[1] See "Mathematical *Truth*?," Chapter 7 of my *Preludes to Pragmatism* (New York: Oxford University Press, 2012). The treatment presented in this chapter will be developed further in forthcoming work.

prefer to link Woolman to Leif Erikson and Priestley/Lavoisier, rather than seeing them as making him look more like Sven Swenson or the root-chewing spirit-mongers and the witch-dunkers?

Nagel and Scanlon might well reply that my examples don't represent the full range of processes underlying discoveries. In many instances, the links between the discoverer and the entities discovered are far less direct. They might point to theoretical science, in which chains of thought lead investigators to recognize previously unsuspected aspects of reality, quite remote from everyday observation. Anticipating that development of their views, I leapt straight to the example of Mendel's discovery of the hereditary factors we now call "genes." Not only did I fail to set that case alongside more straightforward types of discovery, but I also omitted reviewing well-known features of the historical reaction to Mendel. After the rediscovery of his ideas in 1900, the dominant attitude toward his achievement, for at least the first decade or so, was to view him as having supplied a calculational device for predicting how phenotypes would be distributed from different mating patterns. Lacking an adequate conception of what the Mendelian factors might be and how they might affect the observable findings, most early geneticists favored antirealist instrumentalism. Only when it began to become clear how the factors could be considered as particulate entities, whose differences made systematic differences on the phenotypic distribution, did the community convert to realism about genes. Ontological blankness yields epistemological mystery and a retreat from realism.

Srinivasan thinks moral realists might do better by taking up my challenge directly (although she seems dubious about the well-known versions of moral realism). Historians, she thinks, do tell us enough to understand moral progress in realist terms: they point to "Damascene moments" or talk of new "hermeneutical resources" or of "affective engagement with alternative perspectives." Our difference turns on whether those kinds of phrases provide enough, whether they can support the idea that the subjects who undergo such episodes see "through to the normative reality." If that is as far as the historian can go, it appears to me to be too little to support the claims advanced by Nagel and Scanlon, the view of normative reality as constituted by objective reasons (and perhaps Srinivasan would concur with that judgment).

But perhaps it suffices to undergird some generic idea of a realm accurately described by the moral truths.

Reference to "affective engagement with alternative perspectives" is especially promising, since that kind of engagement is apparent in Woolman's conduct—and is taken over in my account of moral method. I agree with Srinivasan that some people "see more deeply and more sensitively than others," that talents of this sort are not evenly distributed across our species, and that those who show the most developed form of these sensitivities are rightly prized (typically retrospectively) as "moral seers." My problem lies in connecting this to the supposed "normative reality." Of course, I understand how such sensitivities help their bearers achieve some insights. By putting them to work, they come to obtain a deep and intimate understanding of the feelings of others and come to recognize how and why those whose psyches they explore adopt certain attitudes and act in particular ways. What isn't evident is how learning things of that sort conveys insight into the grounds of moral truth.

At this point, it's worth asking what prompts philosophers to formulate realist accounts of morality, and why controversies about moral realism arise. Central to pragmatism is William James's worry that philosophical debates are always in danger of collapsing into insignificance because they lose all connection to human action and experience. A lesson I (slowly) learned from Isaac Levi is that realist theses are not worth defending (or attacking) unless they offer methodological advice. Sometimes, by understanding the character of our subject matter, new ways of investigating it are opened up for us. That occurred in the life sciences through the molecular identification of the genetic material, and in historical investigations when scholars came to appreciate the causal roles of social and economic structures. Because the connections between the sympathetic sensitivities apparent in some people who help foster moral advances and the supposed "normative reality" are so opaque, no such benefit accrues from the Discovery View.

So I don't doubt that there are people "who see more deeply and sensitively than others"—but I want a *more* "satisfying account of what makes for such a person" because of my commitment to the Deweyan goal of making moral progress more systematic and sure-footed than it has historically been. This methodological point is not to assimilate moral inquiry to scientific inquiry: to seek *a* method isn't to recommend the *same* method (or, better, given the diversity of the sciences, *kindred* methods). Nor is to "operationalize" something available to all agents. There are two ways to try to advance the Deweyan project. One is to try to help individuals to become *more* sensitive than they might otherwise have been; the other is to introduce social changes to enable a group, with the varied sensitivities distributed among its members, better able to arrive collectively at progressive moral practices. Moral realism would help along the former line, if it were sufficiently linked to the sensitivities Srinivasan and I both recognize in those who introduced new ideas that figured in my examples of moral progress. Because it is so disconnected from the history of moral advance, it simply has nothing to offer.

For philosophers engaged with the projects of contemporary metaethics, abandoning moral realism may appear a retrograde step. Charitably, they may try to understand me as a realist in disguise.[2] Such construals strike me as mistaken. Tempting though it may be to ascribe to me a notion of moral truth—say *Moral truth is what people would agree to under ideal conditions*—that is to misread my opposition to teleology and my view of the proper role of ideals. Instead of thinking of ideals as descriptive of some goal state, I regard them as diagnostic tools, valuable in the *methodological* task of working out how to identify problematic features of current practice and to mark out directions along which we might hope to make immediate advances. So we implement my ideals in practice by making our deliberations *as* inclusive, *as* well-informed, and *as* mutually engaged as we can. Our judgments—of the wrongness of slavery, for example—are counted as true because we take them to have emerged from processes of proper moral inquiry: or, more exactly, from bloody struggles that hew close enough to the contours of proper moral inquiry.[3] In the end, though,

[2] I am grateful to an anonymous referee whose doubts about my departure from moral realism provoked me to state more clearly (but perhaps with too little tact) what I see as a central theme of this book.

[3] Here, evidently, I am recapitulating Dewey's view of truth as what has issued from previous inquiry; of course, it is important that the inquiry be properly carried out. Hence, my more hedged formulation, and the explicit highlighting of the importance of methodology.

whether my position is taken to be some peculiar form of moral realism is a secondary (or tertiary, or . . .) matter. One central point of what I have written here is to change the question. Turning to ontological or semantic questions (the bread and butter of metaethics) promises to help in addressing serious methodological questions: How might we pursue moral inquiry better than we do? Yet, if the semantic or metaphysical discussions offer nothing to help us with these questions, their significance dwindles. Unless, or until, metaethical reflections advance methodology, whether my Deweyan program counts as moral realism or not hardly matters. Perhaps I should have been more forthright from the beginning: moral methodology is central to moral philosophy; semantic and ontological debates are a sideshow.[4]

Methodology, as I conceive it, works at two levels: for individuals and for groups (paradigmatically, societies.) Although I briefly point to potential educational reforms that might encourage greater sensitivity on the part of individuals, the dominant approach of the lectures is to pursue the second, social, strategy. The Deweyan society I envisage, with its institutions for enabling others to hear the cries of the wounded and with its review of ideals of the self, attempts to work with the sensitivities, often limited, of its citizens, by placing them in circumstances where they might exercise the capacities they actually possess: they are asked to confront, directly, the difficulties and sufferings of others. That might be supplemented by efforts to improve individual sensitivity. Many kinds of capacities are unevenly distributed, but people still have opportunities to develop them; they aren't stuck with the luck of the draw. Few of us have absolute pitch, but our ears can be trained.

At the end of her opening section, Srinivasan seems to converge on the position I recommend. She envisages a change in our practices to highlight the perspectives of the disadvantaged. Because she supposes me to endorse the common view of scientific discovery, and to be confined by it in the moral case, she takes there to be a gulf between us. On my conception of the sciences, practice is primary, but the issue

---

[4] Some of Srinivasan's remarks suggest that she is at least somewhat sympathetic to this view. See, in particular, the closing paragraphs of her review of *The Ethical Project*; there are echoes of those paragraphs in her commentary.

is probably better not put in terms of any relation between science and morality. My aim is to begin the process of finding methods for individuals and societies to make moral progress more reliably. One way to read Srinivasan's eloquent brief for advances in moral seeing is as making a rival proposal: instead of the kinds of conversation I envisage, societies ought to amplify the voices of the groups "who call us into a better world." I share the desire to make those voices heard. The difference between us lies in what will be most effective at doing that—and here her emphasis on political power becomes the nub of the disagreement.

Deferring debates about power until the final section, I now want to look more briefly at Srinivasan's second metaethical challenge. She starts from the obvious, but important, point that simply bringing together people with their actual beliefs, attitudes, and habits of discussion would be highly unlikely to achieve any morally valuable outcome. *Actual* conversations between white nationalists and their nonwhite immigrant neighbors don't normally go well. My proposed method, of course, insists on conversations attempting to meet three conditions, and, as Srinivasan rightly recognizes, the affective constraint is crucial: participants should attempt to engage sympathetically and to respect one another. She argues that, to deliver the kinds of conclusions I want, the notions of sympathetic engagement and of mutual respect must be understood as morally charged. Consequently, I haven't supplied an account of moral progress that is free of moral presuppositions. I have made a tacit appeal "to the notion of moral truth."

The challenge is as important as it is familiar. The normative rabbit only emerges from the naturalist's hat because it was surreptitiously inserted in advance. Srinivasan's version is elegant and pithy, deserving a longer treatment than I can offer here. I'll settle for sketching the main lines of my view.

The project of morality, as I understand it, is to devise solutions to a series of problems, affecting human groups from the origin of our species until our ultimate extinction. Those problems stem from a feature of the human condition, namely our being adapted to a particular style of social life, without the psychological capacities that would make living in this way go smoothly and easily. *Homo sapiens*, like our hominin ancestors and our chimpanzee and bonobo cousins, evolved to live in groups mixed by age and sex. That presupposed a capacity, *responsiveness*, for detecting the attitudes of others and adjusting actions to bring us into harmony with those with whom we interact. Because that capacity has been—and remains—limited, its operation is far from perfect. Consequently, we need some device for amplifying our responsiveness. Morality began in extremely simple ways of solving the most dramatic instances of the problem arising in our ancestral environment. Those solutions modified the human social environment, generating new problems, to which new elaborations of morality were then required, and so on in an enormously extended series of changes that have modified human life and human psychology in profound ways.

Looking back on that history, most of whose details are, of course, completely unknown, the naturalistic analyst seeks ways of carrying the project forward on the basis of what has so far been learned. It is a matter, if you like, of improving the device, the responsiveness amplifier. My claims about moral method depend on a diagnosis of the problems the device attempts to resolve (an approach hardly unusual in technological ventures). If I am right that the difficulties lie in failures of responsiveness, then the obvious line of resolution would cultivate the practical stance of exploring the perspectives and motivations of others, seeking to understand what leads them to take the attitudes they do and, at least temporarily, to see the world from their point of view—or from the point of view they would adopt once their factually false beliefs were corrected. Further resolution requires not using any existing asymmetries in situation or in power to impose on any of those involved. At the very beginning of the moral project, some approximation to these practical stances was undertaken, and, throughout its subsequent history, where the project has gone well (resolved, at least partially, the latest forms of the underlying problem), those stances have figured in the thoughts and discussions of participants. The project has been guided by a problem-solving practice, sometimes successful, more often not. The analyst's business is to formulate explicit methods for continuing. Those methods are justified to the extent that they help to address the underlying problems.

Whether this explicit account addresses all the concerns Srinivasan voices—or even whether it counts as "naturalistic"—aren't matters about which I am primarily concerned. She concludes her discussion with two insightful and accurate sentences. My main aim isn't to give "a naturalistic metaphysics of morals" but to offer a progressive way "for going on as a moral community." That is exactly my Deweyan project.

III

Susan Neiman starts with one metaethical question (although she shares my sense that the interest of ontological questions is confined to a small coterie of philosophers). She asks what it was that the abolitionists discovered. The account of the moral project just outlined immediately generates my answer. Moral discovery consists not in fathoming an independent truth ("mapping the realm of reasons") but identifying a problem and (at least partially) solving it. Because the root of the problem lies in our limited responsiveness to one another, it should be no surprise that the pioneers who bring problems to light have been those gifted with the sensitivities Srinivasan rightly celebrates.

Neiman offers a connected series of concerns about my proposals for moral methodology. Her doubts begin in a sober evaluation of the three historical examples I cite. As she observes, the world resulting from the abolition of slavery, the expansion of opportunities for women, and (to a lesser extent) the greater acceptance of same-sex love retains some of the defects of the antecedent state and adds new pathologies. Neiman's daughters "take opportunities for granted" that her generation "had to struggle for," yet, in the light of the objectification to which they are subject and the demands placed on them, they are not convinced of the progressiveness of the change. Her judgment on reactions of this sort is measured: Neiman doesn't endorse the denial of progress, but she is worried.

So am I. To claim that a particular historical episode uncovers a moral problem and partially solves it is not to maintain that the solution is complete. Imperfection comes in three forms: *incompleteness, fragility,* and *mutation.* In all three of my central examples, the response to the marginalized groups was incomplete in two respects, failing to ameliorate the situation of some members of the groups (opportunities restricted to the "talented tenth") and to touch all aspects of life (gay men still have to think hard before joining some social circles). Progress is often fragile in the sense that, without strenuous efforts to maintain what has been accomplished, life will slide back to the former unsatisfactory state (the election of a black president provokes a backlash). Finally, old prejudices and enduring stereotypes emerge in new and unpredictable forms, as in the mutations that trouble Neiman's daughters.

These observations show something important. Moral methodology is needed not only to make further moral progress but also to help preserve, consolidate, and extend the advances already achieved. Sophisticated skeptics about progress conclude that steps forward are inevitably undone by losses, new challenges, and backsliding.[5] Like Neiman, they are correct to identify problems. I take that, however, to be a provocation to address the sources of difficulty, rather than to settle for a forlorn quietism. Indeed, in briefly touching on the sorts of troubles she cites, my second lecture already anticipated my response here.[6]

Yet any serious attempt to maintain and extend advances partially achieved should attend to the underlying forces tending to undo them. Neiman offers a systematic explanation of the troubles to which she has pointed. Capitalism is to blame. While I sympathize with her diagnosis, it strikes me as too simple. First, "capitalism" is an umbrella term, covering a large number of ways in which economic practices (and broader social practices) can be bundled together. A particular *style* of capitalism, one hostile to social (and moral) constraints on the pursuit of profit and widely dominant in the world today, is indeed inimical to moral progress. To recognize that should not lead one to abandon the idea that markets sometimes help in solving social problems. As Alvin Roth emphasizes, markets can be adapted to achieve a wide variety

---

[5] See, for example, John Gray, *Seven Types of Atheism* (New York: Farrar, Straus, Giroux, 2018).

[6] See the closing section of Chapter 2.

of goals, if they are thoughtfully designed and constructed.[7] Second, a purely economic diagnosis fails to recognize the pervasive role of stereotypes and stigmatization in undermining, and even in undoing, moral advances. I don't doubt that economic pressures reinforce xenophobia, pernicious forms of nationalism, and racism, but they work in tandem with the effects studied by psychologists (Claude Steele) and economists(!) like Glenn Loury.[8]

My lectures already suggest the lines along which I would seek to address Neiman's concerns. The coda to Chapter 3 takes a brief look at how the methodology I propose might be applied in the world today: Where are *our* blind spots? Three out of my four long-term suggestions concern the distribution of the resources people need, the debasement of ideals of the self resulting from overemphasis on productivity, and the erosion of community caused by the insistence on unrestrained competition.[9] In all three instances, I am questioning central features of the capitalism practiced in our age. As my brief remarks about education in section IV of Chapter 3 indicate, I also envisage educational reforms designed to promote greater fluency in the sensitivities and skills required for participating in ideal conversation. More explicitly, I propose that early childhood education should involve sequential practice in joint planning, in which young people will constantly be led on to interact with, and to find ways of cooperating with, others with whom they form ever more diverse groups.[10] Experiments in facilitating these kinds of encounters would aim at eradicating stereotypes and forestalling tendencies to stigmatize.

So far, I have agreed with Neiman's concerns about the three historical examples, construed them as a call to apply my proposed methodology to the outcomes of these episodes, partially endorsed her diagnosis of the source of the underlying difficulty, and thus directed the application toward a (clarified) target. At this point, our strategies

---

[7] See his Nobel Lecture, available at http://www.nobelprize.org/nobel_prizes/economic-sciences/laureates/2012/roth-lecture.html.

[8] Claude Steele, *Whistling Vivaldi* (New York: Norton, 2010); Glenn Loury, *The Anatomy of Racial Inequality* (Cambridge, MA: Harvard University Press, 2002).

[9] See p. 75.

[10] This proposal is elaborated and defended in *The Main Enterprise of the World*. See Chapter 3, note 14.

start to diverge. For Neiman thinks I place too much weight on the cognitive, and that I overestimate the reasonableness of human beings. (This is already present in the charming compliment she pays in the first paragraph of her commentary.) I plead not guilty. Helping people reason more cogently, think more clearly, and become better informed is important for the improvement of moral discussion, but it cannot be the whole story. Indeed, as Srinivasan recognizes, sympathetic engagement with others is crucial to the deliberations I commend.

Neiman characterizes Woolman's moral inquiry in cognitive terms—and perhaps my accounts of his pioneering efforts are to blame for this interpretation. Although his *Journal* is pervaded by a sense of piety and religious duty, it is hard to believe that Woolman could have committed himself so thoroughly to efforts to persuade slave owners, especially his fellow Quakers, to abandon the practice, without sympathy for the sufferings of the slaves and a corresponding emotional revulsion against slaveholding. His devotion to the cause involved long journeys, frequently marked by bouts of sickness. As he ranged far and wide, the scope of his mission expanded, embracing the plight of native Americans and, eventually, the poor and marginalized in any community; this is particularly evident in the entries from England, in the visit that preceded his death, far from home and family. Sympathy is explicitly expressed in occasional passages, in his pleas to cultivate a "spirit of tenderness" toward the slaves and to "use them kindly," in his confession that to record how slaves are typically treated is "no agreeable work," culminating in a reminder that these are "souls for whom Christ died," and his self-description of being drawn into "a sympathizing tenderness with the sheep of Christ, however distinguished from one another in this world."[11]

People are inclined, of course, to suppress information that might call into question their conduct and their habits. Neiman thinks that this occurred in the practice of slavery in the New World. Here, I think, the historical details tell against her. To be sure, the Portuguese and Spanish recognized facts about African culture that Cotton Mather and his interlocutors denied. Yet by what channel would the information

---

[11] John Woolman, *The Journal of John Woolman* (New York: Citadel Press, 1961), 54, 59, 60, 95.

have flowed to fanatical Puritans, whose original homeland had been threatened by the Spanish, and for whom the Catholicism of the Iberian Peninsula was even more repugnant than the mild compromise Protestantism driving them to cross the Atlantic? By the period in which the North American colonies were stocked with slaves from Africa, the suppliers were effectively kidnapping Africans from the interior, bringing them to the coast for sale to enterprising sea captains. It isn't hard to envisage how the sellers portrayed their victims to the potential buyers, and how, even if they came to believe differently, those who transported slaves to North America would have refrained from subverting views of their wares as other than savages. If anything is clear about Cotton Mather and his fellow settlers, it is that considerations of economic profit are not comparable to the urge to merit salvation.

As the practice of slaveholding expanded, the thought of the masters as bringing their slaves to the gates of heaven certainly receded and faded away. Yet the stereotype of the Africans as savages, whose mental capacities and emotional sensitivities are vastly inferior to those of Anglo-Saxons remained. Neiman rightly asks "how empathy was so successfully suppressed." Slaves, she points out, "presided over the most intimate and vulnerable aspects of slaveholders' lives." Her question—Lear's question: Is there any cause in nature that makes these hard hearts?—is a good one. For, if people are, by some aspect of human nature, led always to suppress sympathy when it opposes their selfish interests, the kinds of conversations envisaged by my moral methodology are doomed to failure.

This, I believe, is the center of our disagreement. Human responsiveness is limited, and the moral project is dedicated to amplifying it. Moral methodology searches for circumstances under which the limits are relaxed. At the core of my proposal is the thought that bringing people together to explain themselves to one another, enjoining them to search for mutual understanding, providing opportunities for them to relate their own needs, lacks, and sufferings, can trigger the capacities for sympathy they actually have. People with very different perspectives can come to understand the world from others' standpoints, temporarily trying on one another's lives to see how they fit. Experiments in arranging discussions, similar in some respects to the type I favor, offer some encouragement.[12] Mutual engagement is possible, at least to some extent. How far it can go is as yet unknown.

Neiman's powerful example of the slave owners who withheld sympathy from the house slaves who assisted them in intimate aspects of their lives appears to offer evidence for drawing a boundary. If, under those historical circumstances, people could be so unfeeling, why should anyone trust in any possibility of creating the kinds of discussions I recommend? To my mind, the trouble lay in the persistence of stereotypes. *Uncle Tom's Cabin* may not be a literary masterpiece, but, in many instances, Harriet Beecher Stowe reveals a penetrating psychological intelligence. Her portrait of Marie St. Clare, attuned to her own complaints, and correspondingly dismissive of the difficulties felt by those around her, shows how actions are assessed through prevalent myths of racial difference. Those who serve her are cruder folk, incapable of the delicate sensibilities with which she is afflicted. She who has lived her life in the world of plantation slavery understands the character of the slaves far better than her well-meaning (but ultimately feckless) husband. Her "experience," we are led to believe, is a matter of absorption of the tradition of negro savagery, and it prompts her to the unfeeling judgments she makes about the dedicated people who minister to her and to her kin in the most intimate aspects of their lives. Nor can one dismiss Marie as an imaginative fiction, a caricature. The language she employs and the attitudes she expresses are found in the sober prose of eminent men, Thomas Jefferson prominent among them.[13]

Overcoming the barriers to extended responsiveness may sometimes, even often, require modifying the economic order of society (amending capitalism) so as to diminish the pressures to satisfy selfish preferences. Not, however, in this case. Here the trouble lies

[12] One program that has achieved some successes is that of James Fishkin; see his *When the People Speak* (New York: Oxford University Press, 2009). Another is a Duke University program, the North Carolina Forum (about which I learned from Leslie Winner, one of its leading organizers). For a detailed account of how constructive exchanges across political divides (chasms) become possible, see also Arlie Russell Hochschild, *Strangers in Their Own Land: Anger and Mourning on the American Right* (New York: The New Press, 2016).

[13] See note 5 to Chapter 2, and the reference to Query 14 of Jefferson's *Notes on the State of Virginia*.

in the origination and perpetuation of stereotypes. Even in the mid-nineteenth-century, Frederick Douglass's hearers were not willing to modify their views about the intelligence of slaves. Until his famous demonstration, they preferred to deny that he had once been enslaved. Neiman senses the point, when she connects failures of empathy with the notion of false consciousness. As I defined that concept, false consciousness occurs when marginalized people accept views about themselves and the suitable course of their lives prescribed for them by an oppressive ambient society. If I read her correctly, Neiman recognizes the kinship between this narrow concept and a broader one, covering instances of distorted vision on the part of the oppressors.

Breaking down stereotypes is hard. Even when an African American president and his family behave with dignity and grace throughout eight years, even when his decisions are plainly marked with thought and intelligence and genuine concern for the public good, even when he is succeeded by a man whose personal conduct would, for almost all of American history, have aroused unanimous scorn, derision, and irate denunciation, a man whose lack of concern for anything but his own advancement is striking, a significant part of the American public remains convinced that white people are, by nature, morally and intellectually superior to their black and brown fellows. Lear's question is an important one, and, in the present American political context, our lack of a full answer is evident. Yet incomplete knowledge isn't total ignorance. Enough is known about factors that reinforce stereotypes to suggest ways of combating them. When people feel that their ways of living are threatened, and might collapse entirely if certain beliefs are abandoned, they are often inclined to resist evidence. Combining demonstration of equality across racial lines with social reassurance might not eliminate stereotypes entirely, but it might weaken them enough to dislodge the more pernicious forms of false consciousness (in the broader sense).

Hence, I'm not willing to conclude that achieving the sympathy required for implementing my proposed moral methodology is hopeless. The issues here are ultimately empirical, and, given the understanding of the role of stereotypes currently available, there are options to explore. So I take Neiman to have issued an important challenge in calling attention to the tendency to suppress sympathy, but I deny that we have good reason to think it an insuperable one.

Her critique concludes with an alternative suggestion. Perhaps, she suggests, we can look elsewhere for ways of tapping human emotions to promote moral progress. As she points out, in one of the few philosophical attempts to tackle questions of moral change by looking at human history, Anthony Appiah invokes the notion of honor as a potential motor of moral progress. Wary of my attempts to build on sympathy, to foster mutual engagement, Neiman considers the possibilities of harnessing our egoistic sentiments. Human beings crave esteem. Perhaps the concept of honor can point them to paths of moral improvement?

Like Neiman, I am an admirer of Appiah's work, and of *The Honor Code*. That book shows, very convincingly how, *given a particular kind of context*, the yearning for honor can be a powerful weapon for moral change. Yet, toward the end of her discussion of his views, Neiman acknowledges a problem Appiah explicitly recognizes. Honor is like the weaponry of a mercenary army: the guns are not destined to point in any particular direction. In many societies, including some contemporary ones, codes of honor have been invoked to do hideous things, to kill the women who have dishonored the clan or the tribe, to motivate aggression for trivial or imaginary offenses, to perpetuate stereotypes of masculinity, and on and on and on. Appiah's discussions should be read beside those of Shakespeare's great skeptics about honor (Falstaff and Parolles), in combination with Arthur Schnitzler's scathing novella, *Leutnant Gustl*, and beside the everyday reports of school bullying, gang culture, and the forced marriages of girls to their rapists.

If the aim is to make moral progress more systematic and sure-footed, honor will not serve. To be sure, *when human sympathy has been achieved and the direction of change recognized*, honor may be enlisted to help facilitate moral progress. Without something that will do the work of my moral methodology, honor is impotent. Hence, to sum up my reply to Neiman, I don't see any serious alternative to the approach I have proposed. Plainly there is much work to be done to overcome the barriers to human sympathy—the limits of our natural responsiveness to others are, of course, at the root of my account of the moral project. But, I submit, the Deweyan aim is a valuable one, and, while there are chances of making progress with respect to it, we are well-advised to try.

Neiman concludes her commentary with the thought of giving moral progress more allure. Following a suggestion of Srinivasan's, she proposes advertising moral deliberation as "woke." Although I don't view myself as having much in common with Cotton Mather, perhaps I retain a Puritan streak. Flashy slogans on behalf of moral progress strike me as dangerously counterproductive. Not only do they need constant renewal—today's "woke" is tomorrow's "with it" or maybe "awesome"—but they are at odds with the spirit of moral delibera-tion. If the hidden persuaders entice fashion-conscious people to think about moral questions, the end result seems more likely to be an exer-cise in posturing rather than a serious confrontation with the issues.

IV

One of the great pleasures of my philosophical reading in recent years has been the discovery of Rahel Jaeggi's work. As she correctly notes, there are close affinities in our choices of problems and our strategies for addressing them. To find such close connections between views derived from very different philosophical traditions is deeply encouraging.

Yet, as Jaeggi also sees, the differences between Frankfurt-style crit-ical theory (especially in the mode practiced by Axel Honneth and herself) and my Deweyan pragmatism sometimes matter. In the end, I don't think it's the *cognitivism* of my approach that is the source of the important disagreements—as I've tried to explain earlier, the ampli-fication of *empathetic* understanding lies at the heart of my method-ology.[14] The root of the trouble is my "neglect of the socio-structural as well as historical dimension of the problems." Despite my efforts to treat individuals as inevitably socially situated, and to deal with moral progress at both the individual and the social level without supposing that the social is ultimately reducible to the individual, philosophers

[14] See the discussion of Neiman's charge that I overemphasize the cognitive.

trained in the tradition that leads from Hegel and Marx to contemporary critical theory and German social philosophy will detect at least a whiff of methodological individualism in some of my formulations.

As I have discovered, it is not easy for those of us brought up in a culture in which methodological individualism dominates to break entirely free from its influence.[15] The Anglophone ear needs training— and I am not confident that my own training has yet gone far enough. Hence, although I shall try to show how I accommodate the "sociostructural," in the guises Jaeggi presents, I envisage the possibility that something may still be missing. My hope, however, is that, in attempting to be clear about these difficult matters, she and I may make further progress and, perhaps, achieve closer convergence.

Her initial charge is that my account of problems is too subjective. I agree completely with Dewey's claim that it's the situation that counts as problematic. The analysis offered in my lectures distinguishes between cases in which people think there's a problem and problematic situations. *Objectively* problematic situations, I propose, are those justifiably counted as problematic "in the long run and on the whole." Plainly, I am taking over the approach to truth and reality pioneered by Peirce and James, and taken over by Dewey. To see that as oversubjective is to adopt a more demanding sense of objectivity, one that treats "is problematic" as applying to situations independently of the responses of subjects to them. In my view, that is to demand too much.

Jaeggi's way of specifying the property of being problematic is to locate it in "moments of crisis and dysfunction." I have no objection to the use of those terms, but I don't see how they can be given any clear sense except insofar as they are linked to "obstacles and hindrances" within human affairs. Situations are, apparently, problematic *for particular historical agents* or *for particular social configurations*. Slavery, we might say, was problematic in virtue of its blighting of human lives and its production of an inevitably unstable system of social relations.

---

[15] This was vividly brought home to me during a valuable workshop Jaeggi organized at the New School in New York. Dick Bernstein, Jay Bernstein, Axel Honneth, and Jaeggi herself all pointed out—correctly—how my presentation had turned individualistic at crucial moments. I strongly doubt that any of the orthodox Anglo-American philosophers present noticed.

What would count as a problematic situation (period)? One whose status as problematic never had anything to do with the confined lives of human beings? Perhaps Jaeggi would declare that the inevitable instability of the social relations is enough to mark situations generating them as problematic, whether or not any particular people suffer. But why should anyone think that inevitable instability can occur in the absence of reformers who are prodded into action by the difficulties faced by some of their fellows? The demand for some notion of objectivity unmoored to any human suffering or limitations on human lives looks impossible to meet. Hence, I suggest, the pragmatist approach to problems yields objectivity enough.

Yet her worries about the objectivity of my concept of a problem are only the curtain-raiser to Jaeggi's main line of criticism. In discussing the "embeddedness" of moral practices, she points to phenomena that the methodology developed in the lectures is ill-equipped to handle. One way for me to respond would be to reiterate my point about the preliminary character of the methods I propose. It's conceded, from the beginning, that the proposals are just the start of the enterprise, and that methods will be extended, refined, reformed, modified, and sometimes discarded as more and more modes of moral progress come within the purview of future analysts. The criticism would thus be portrayed as a "friendly amendment" (Jaeggi's term) to the project I have recommended.

To stop there would, however, be to underrate the importance of the concern. For the phenomena singled out by Jaeggi are close enough to the historical examples I deploy and, simultaneously, expose a narrowness—an *individualistic* narrowness—in the perspective of the lectures. So I see her challenge as an opportunity to expand the framework I have offered.

The example of marital rape is completely apt for making Jaeggi's point. Why was marital rape invisible (and not just in Germany) for so long? Historians can only guess at the percentage of married women who have sometimes been coerced into having sex with their husbands when they were completely disinclined. Even without data, it's reasonable to estimate that the percentage is far from insignificant. Did women in this group feel "wounded"? Probably not. Except for those who were roughly compelled into submission, they may well have

felt this to be a (regrettable) part of wifely duty. The false consciousness present here can't be assimilated to my talk of ideals of the self,
allowed to some but not to others. My discussions of the expansion
of opportunities for women envisage—and work best for—different
cases: women's abilities to own property, to vote, to be educated, to
enter certain kind of professions. The idea of a "right to say no" or the
ideal of sex as initiated through joint agreement doesn't belong within
the conception of marriage that once ran through a complex of institutional and cultural practices. Only when that complex begins to break
up is it possible to recognize male coercion of wifely sex as a problem
to be addressed.

Societies organize the lives of those who live in them in all sorts
of domains. Interlocking institutions—marriage, the raising of children, the workplace, the economy, religion, the law—generate roles
that people assume, and, in consequence, those people acquiesce in
conventions and norms. Deviation becomes unthinkable. Then, at
some historical moment, a change, quite possibly of some remote type,
disturbs the interconnections, exposing options that had previously
been hidden. Technology, or a war, forces habits and routines to be
abandoned, raising, for the first time, questions about what behavior is
appropriate to a familiar situation.[16]

Any extension of my proposed moral methodology requires understanding two socio-structural concepts: *institutional fit* and its con-
verse *institutional friction*. The idea that institutions that appear to be
making progress in their own terms can combine to produce a disastrous regression should be thoroughly familiar. Think of the often-
fraught relationship among technology, economic productivity, and
the environment or the impact of economic efficiency on education.
To take the Deweyan project of making moral progress more systematic and sure-footed seriously thus faces a challenge: how, given the apparent fit among institutions, can one identify in advance the problems
that would be exposed if and when institutional friction disrupts the
current situation? Must societies simply wait to see what their future
development brings, without any prospect of recognizing in advance

---

[16] Such possibilities lie behind John MacFarlane's deep question about the role of
technology in the moral revolutions I discuss. See Chapter 3, section II.

what will later be viewed as serious deficiencies (like coercive sex in the marriage bed)? Do we have to wait for history, or can we hasten it?

Jaeggi's own answer to these questions may be the pessimistic one: Nothing to be done. That is suggested by her explanation of Oscar Wilde's failure. "The time was not ripe." Here, I side with Marx, rather than with Hegel. Human beings, aided by probing analyses of social structures, can anticipate the problems and accelerate progress. The conversationalists I envisage can explore the ways in which the current interlocking of institutions generates particular assumptions about proper roles, going on to ask what might be possible, or valuable, if those assumptions were rescinded, and how the various groups represented in the deliberation might gain thereby. Rather than adopting an individualistic approach to ideals of the self, treating those ideals singly, as my discussion of false consciousness does, they can try to search out the ways in which the present institutional structure makes certain ways of living beyond the conceptual horizons of some kinds of people, and thus currently confines those people's lives. (So there *is* an individualistic blind spot in my treatment of false consciousness; but it isn't standard methodological individualism, but an atomistic view of social identities and ideals of the self.)

A number of qualifications and caveats are needed. First, I've tried to reinterpret Jaeggi's principal illustration, embedding it within the approach offered in the lectures. Even assuming that I have done justice to the example of marital rape, it doesn't follow that all phenomena requiring a socio-cultural perspective can be assimilated in the same way, or that there are no instances requiring a more radical change of framework. I hope, however, that considering this concrete case gives substance to the general strategy of developing further my embryonic methodology, and thus reveals how Jaeggi's critique might be considered as a "friendly amendment."

Second, she might object that the role I envisage for the kinds of deliberations central to my methodological proposals continues to reflect the style of individualism from which she tries to liberate me. Yet, however sensitive one may be to holistic social considerations, I don't see how to avoid returning, in the end, to the impact that social changes have on individual lives. Partly, this is a consequence of the claims

I have made in response to her charges of subjectivism: situations are problematic because, in the end, they have negative impacts on people. Beyond that is a Deweyan point. If moral progress is to become more systematic and sure-footed, that isn't going to happen by discovering some new magic. I don't believe in spells to treat social pathologies (and, I suspect, Rahel doesn't either). Although it may be achieved through amplification of empathy, reliable moral progress is bound to have a cognitive dimension. The changes that relieve human confinement, where not lucky accidents of history, occur because individual agents recognize suffering or confinement they have failed to see before, and then act on the basis of their new understanding. If a probing social analysis discloses the assumptions about proper roles latent in the current patterns of interlocking institutions, the *status* of those assumptions—as problematic or benign—cannot be determined without the kinds of explorations my deliberations envisage. An inclusive group of well-informed people must consider how those assumptions affect one another's lives, and whether it is possible that abandoning those assumptions might prove liberating. Without that kind of collective pondering, it's hard to see any alternative to the messy, contingent processes that have generated the kinds of moral progress identifiable in the past.

Third, as with the (limited) kind of false consciousness considered in Lecture 2, social experimentation will probably be needed if the excavation of taken-for-granted assumptions is to direct change. Recognizing how the institution of marriage has packaged together various forms of behavior appropriate to the wifely role, women, and any men who sympathize with them, might come to recognize problematic pressures in the marriage bed. Consequently, they may seek an alternative conception of marriage, more egalitarian in character. They cannot, however, know in advance whether the elaborations of marital roles they envisage will solve the problem without sacrificing other values they cherish. I conjecture that the ethical issues surrounding the conduct of the necessary trials—experiments that those inspired by the uncovering of latent assumptions are justified in pursuing—are even more delicate than in the more restricted examples of false consciousness. Precisely because of the interlocking patterns of social institutions, the effects of change are likely to be felt on a larger scale.

Fourth, the proposal to probe the fit among domains of human life recalls the Deweyan conception of philosophy as responding to the practices of the age—the state of knowledge, of social and political affairs, of norms and values, of patterns of conduct and belief—and striving for a synthetic understanding of its "meanings."[17] The understanding of institutional fit (and institutional friction) is plainly a large part of this philosophical endeavor. Jaeggi's discussion is a vivid reminder of the ways in which the tradition of critical theory, from Marx on, has pursued such understanding. My emphasis on recognizing the hidden assumptions about roles (and my reference to excavation) suggests another unexpected kinship. Genealogy, as conceived by Nietzsche and Foucault, is also pertinent. Deweyan pragmatism should embrace traditions with which it is not usually associated.[18] (So, as Jaeggi also reminds me, there's a "historical dimension" that my lectures didn't consider explicitly.)

Fifth, and finally, attempts to probe the social structures might be so unreliable, or the enterprise of uncovering and pondering latent assumptions might yield no insights into progressive change, or the consequent activities of exploring alternative conceptions of roles might prove so costly in terms of the suffering they bring, that societies would do better by abandoning the attempt to make moral progress of this sort more systematic and sure-footed. We would simply have to wait for the time to be ripe. Efforts to hasten history are beyond our abilities. Acquiescing in pessimism would offer a Pyrrhic victory for the methodology I have proposed. The suggestions of the Lectures offer ways to try to improve the prospects of moral progress—in a

[17] I discuss Dewey's view of philosophy in "Dewey's Conception of Philosophy" (Chapter 1 of Steven Fesmire, ed., *The Oxford Handbook of Dewey* (New York: Oxford University Press, 2019), 3–21. There are obvious affinities with Wilfrid Sellars's famous characterization: "The aim of philosophy, abstractly formulated, is to understand how things in the broadest sense of the term hang together in the broadest sense of the term" ("Philosophy and the Scientific Image of Man," Chapter 1 of *Science, Perception, and Reality* (London: Routledge & Kegan Paul, 1963), 1.
[18] I explore this theme at greater length in "John Dewey Goes to Frankfurt" (see the end of note 46 to Chapter 2 above).

restricted domain. If, however, we try to extend them to the complex social instances to which Jaeggi rightly points, it turns out that nothing can be done.

But why give up in advance? I prefer to make a larger concession to Jaeggi's critique. She is correct to see my methodology as needing extension. In reply, I've attempted to sketch how that extension might go.

V

My commentators take me to err in reading the history of moral progress. The emphasis on discussion and on mutual sympathy is too far from the realities of the struggles out of which advances actually occurred. Srinivasan puts the point with exemplary clarity and force: "the history of much moral progress has not been fundamentally a history of conversation at all, but a history of power: the wielding of power by the dominant against the oppressed, and the eventual seizing of that power, or some small part of that power, by the dominated." Nobody should overlook or downplay the courage of those who were reviled and beaten and wounded and killed in the efforts to alleviate the plight of the oppressed.

I agree. Completely. Struggles for power—violent struggles— are central to the *actual* histories of the episodes I have chosen as paradigms. They may well have been features of all *past* major moral advances. That is a point from which I begin. My Deweyan project is to seek conditions, reformed institutions based on revised understandings of moral progress, that might facilitate progressive change with less need for violence. As I understand the position shared by my commentators (and by other philosophers whom I admire[19]), it views this venture as undermined by the lessons of history. Realistic champions of moral progress will suppose that violent contestation of power will always be integral to going forward. Even when those who

---

[19] See, for example, Chapter 5 of Elizabeth Anderson, *The Imperative of Integration* (Princeton, NJ: Princeton University Press, 2010), where Anderson recognizes the importance of demonstrations as a form of speech to promote moral advances.

demand the change use only the tools of passive resistance, eschewing violence, they will still be made to suffer.

For those with Deweyan hopes, this "realism" appears as pessimism. The *Pessimistic Thesis* can take one of a number of forms. I'll just distinguish the strongest and the weakest versions.

> *Weak Pessimism.* In at least some instances of attempts to make moral progress, it will be impossible to eradicate completely the role of power and violent contestation of power.

> *Strong Pessimism.* In all instances of attempts to make moral progress, it will be impossible to diminish the role of power and violent contestation of power below the level present in the historical examples.

Similarly, someone who sympathizes with Dewey's goal might be more or less optimistic.

> *Weak Optimism.* In at least some instances of attempts to make moral progress, the institutions of a Deweyan society would diminish the role of power and violent contestation of power below the level present in the historical examples.

> *Strong Optimism.* In all instances of attempts to make moral progress, the institutions of a Deweyan society would eradicate completely the role of power and violent contestation of power.

Strong Optimism is incompatible with all forms of Pessimism; Strong Pessimism is incompatible with all forms of Optimism; Weak Optimism and Weak Pessimism are entirely consistent with one another.[20]

Pessimists tend to view optimists as unworldly dreamers. Optimists see pessimists as gloomily giving up too easily. To my mind, *both* strong

---

[20] It's fairly straightforward to construct intermediate versions of Pessimism and Optimism; some pairs of the intermediate positions are mutually consistent; others are not.

positions appear as unsupported dogma. The extent of our ability to facilitate moral progress through peaceful means is simply unknown. History doesn't decide among the theses—although it may make us hesitant about *either* of the strong versions.

I start from the conviction that even achieving a state in which Weak Optimism were realized would be valuable. Even if the recourse to political struggles will always be necessary, if the methodological proposals I have made diminished the bloodshed and the chanciness of some future moral advances, they would be worth having. At this juncture, it is impossible to tell how much good they might achieve. Perhaps in some important instances the institutionalization of inquiry into the cries of the wounded might even sidestep entirely the need for politics and any attendant violence. We cannot know if we do not try. My—pragmatist—proposal is to act on the basis of Weak Optimism and to push as far as we can. This is by no means to deny to the oppressed the weapons they have typically used in trying to change the conditions of their lives, but to see them as a last resort when the institutions for airing and assessing their grievances have failed.

Political power is, of course, unevenly distributed. Optimists hope to create social conditions in which decision-making is more egalitarian. A principal lesson from history, a point on which my commentators and I all agree, is that the maldistribution of power creates conditions under which the wounded are not heard and their sufferings are undiminished. Only when they start to fight for power are their voices heard, and, consequently, their plight is sometimes (occasionally?) relieved. Dewey's question asks whether it is possible to do better than that. My aim is to reform our social frameworks to provide ways of moral advance through less violent means—to make automatic and assured what is currently fought for under disadvantageous political conditions. History provides no impossibility proof. Why not try?

Perhaps because methodological proposals may appear to be at odds with ineradicable features of human life.[21] Inequalities of power will inevitably infect the actual discussions people have. Conversation will thus fall so far short of the ideal conditions I present that it will

---

[21] I am extremely grateful to an anonymous referee who astutely posed the sharp version of my commentators' challenge considered in this paragraph.

fail to respond to the cries of the wounded. I want institutionalized discussions, set up with real people (who will be unequally powerful and will be variously prejudiced), under the aegis of my ideals, used as diagnostic tools. Take ordinary folk and ask them to discuss—but tell them how important it is to represent all points of view, to rely only on what can be supported by evidence, and to try to engage with one another's perspectives.[22] Will explaining those rules of deliberation help? The problem is, I suggest a practical one. How best to find representatives of different perspectives who can meet one another on something like the terms of mutual engagement? If John Calhoun is selected as a representative of slaveholding, a fair bit of preliminary work is likely to be needed if he is to listen seriously to Frederick Douglass and to enter sympathetically into the lives of slaves.[23] If no amount of preliminary work will do the trick, Calhoun must give way to some less closed-minded discussant, one who, nonetheless, initially shares his belief in the defensibility of slavery. Several experiments in equalizing democratic deliberation have been tried,[24] and we still have much to explore before deciding which frameworks function best— just as Galileo and his peers faced many questions in their attempts to apply their inchoate methods of inquiry. Would educational reforms, for example, dissolve prejudices and weaken tendencies to dominate, so that potential deliberators were more likely to accord with the conversational conditions?[25]

A concluding fantasy. It is 2250. Miraculously, our planet has survived the climate crisis, and sustainable forms of human life, retaining the better features of contemporary existence, remain possible. During the intervening period, Deweyan moral inquiry has developed and been integrated into all human societies. Historians reflect on what that has achieved. One of them draws an interesting parallel.

---

[22] Of course, jurors are instructed to reflect in ways that often diverge from their everyday habits. Should we suppose those instructions always to be ineffective?

[23] I owe this vivid example to Robert Gooding-Williams, who independently formulated the referee's concern.

[24] See the references cited in note 12 earlier.

[25] In *The Main Enterprise of the World* (see above, Chapter 3, note 14), I try to elaborate and defend this possibility.

In the twenty-first century, the move to facilitate moral progress through institutions for mutually engaged deliberation was often criticized by gloomy naysayers who supposed that the bloody struggles for power were indispensable to moral advance. We can now see that the reform of society envisaged by Dewey and those whom he influenced was akin to the construction of the system of justice as Locke imagined it. From a preceding condition in which asymmetries of strength and power determined the outcome of social conflicts, the state emerged to provide a forum in which rival claims could be heard. We can extend Locke's speculative story[26] by introducing figures who doubted whether the struggles among rival clans and coalitions could ever be replaced by anything superior— they would have been the pessimists (or, as they would have preferred it: realists) of their day. Appealing to the historical record, they castigated those who argued for institutionalized courts and procedures as romantic dreamers. Just as they were defeated by the successes (typically incomplete and hard-won) of the program favored by their opponents, so too the naysayers of the twenty-first century have been refuted by the progress made in the methodology of moral inquiry. We should be grateful that some of the "dreamers" refused to give up.

A fantasy is not, of course, an argument. It may, however, supply a perspective. Amia, Susan, and Rahel have raised important questions about the viability of the enterprise I have tried to launch here. There are no guarantees that it will not flounder, and that, in retrospect, those who attempt to contribute to it will not appear as muddled idealists. But, despite my admiration for my commentators, I am not persuaded that the venture should be abandoned as hopeless.

---

[26] See Locke's *Second Treatise of Government*, Chapter 3 (in John Locke, *Political Writings*, edited by David Wootton [Indianapolis: Hackett, 2003]).

Index

For the benefit of digital users, indexed terms that span two pages (e.g., 52–53) may, on occasion, appear on only one of those pages.

abolitionism, 13, 19–20, 23, 43, 44, 45, 58–59, 80, 81–82, 90, 104, 112, 114, 115–17, 123–24, 134, 149
achievement (moral, social, political), 33–34, 53, 74–75, 86–87, 89, 95–96, 109, 128
  social accomplishment, 53–54, 96, 100
admiration, 53–54
Africa(n), 41–43, 44, 114–15, 152–53
agency, moral, 53–54, 105
altruism, 50n.15, 127
America, 81, 112–13, 115–16, 139, 141, 152–53, 155
  African American, 112, 115–16, 155
  native American, 152
American Civil War, 14n.2, 44, 80–81
ancient Greece, 61–63
anthropology, 56–57, 141–42
Appiah, Kwame Anthony, 116–18, 156
appraisal, moral, 88, 94
appropriateness, 34–35, 37
authority, moral, 45n.10, 57–59, 106–7
automatism, 34, 88–89, 90, 133–34
autonomy, 66–67, 68–69, 71, 99. *See also* freedom
awareness, moral, 16–17, 29, 84–85, 96–97, 126–27, 130–31

Beecher Stowe, Harriet, 115–16, 154
beliefs, moral, 15–16, 17–18, 82–85, 86–87, 90–91, 95–96, 97–98
Berkeleyan view, 26–28, 34, 122
bias, implicit, 126, 128
blindness, moral, 13, 29, 30–31, 33, 99, 116, 151, 161

bullying, 156
burden, moral, 35–36, 46–47, 59, 95–96

Calhoun, John, 166–67
capitalism, 113–14, 150–51, 154–55
Catholicism, 21–22, 42n.2, 152–53
causality, 53, 54, 56
change, moral, 32, 44, 81–82, 91, 103, 105, 109–10, 131, 132
  change within change, 129
Christianity, 45n.10, 114–15
civil rights, 109–10
climate change, 81, 86–87, 100, 167
code, moral, 45n.9, 57, 90, 93–94, 95–96
cognition, moral. *See* cognitivism
cognitivism, 15–16, 17, 21, 73–75, 113–14. *See also* metaethics; noncognitivism
Coke, Sir Edward, 33
Colonialism, 109–10
community, 35, 39, 63–64, 65, 66–67, 71–72, 73–74, 77–78, 88, 99–100, 108–9, 111, 123, 128, 135, 151
competition, 99–100, 151
complicity, 43
conflict, moral, 75, 85, 113, 123–24, 126–28, 168
consciousness, false, 30, 33, 41–72, 116, 122, 125, 126, 127–28, 154–55, 159–60, 161, 162–63
conservatism, 96–97
constructivism, 37–38n.24, 122–23
contractualism, democratic, 38, 55–56, 57–58, 75, 109

conversation, 33–40
    ideal conversation, 34, 37–38, 44,
        47–48, 88–89, 92–93, 97, 107–8, 110,
        123, 126, 151
    public conversation, 33–34, 45, 109
cooperation, 50–52, 119, 120, 123–24,
    127, 132–33
correctness, political, 14
creativity, ethical, 104–5
crisis, 119–36, 158–59
critical theory, 71–72n.46, 157–58, 163

Damascene moments, 104, 143–44
Darwin, Charles, 31–32, 81
deafness, moral, 30, 41, 59, 111, 114. See
    also moral blindness
decision(-making), moral, 38–39, 58,
    108–9, 110
deliberation, ideal, 81, 88–89, 98. See also
    ideal conversation
democracy, 37, 57, 58, 110, 134–35, 166–67
deontology, 135–36
determinism, 132, 133–34
Dewey, John, 14–15, 31–32, 79, 92–93,
    122–23, 125, 135–36, 158, 166, 168
    Deweyan pragmatism, 15–16, 38–39,
        47–48, 144–46, 157–58, 163
    Deweyan society, 96–98, 134–35,
        146, 165
diagnostic tool, 28–29, 145–46, 166–67
directive, moral, 30–32, 84–85
discovery, moral, 20, 21, 28, 56–57, 73,
    74–75, 78–79, 105, 106–7, 149
    discovery view, 15–18, 20–21, 25–26,
        28, 56–57, 73, 74–75, 79, 80, 103–6,
        107, 111–12, 120, 129, 135, 139–
        40, 144
discrimination, 28–29, 77–78, 112–13,
    121, 142–43
dissident voices, 33–34, 109
division of labor, 54, 62, 126–27
domination, 48, 109–10, 121, 123–24,
    126–27, 130, 164, 166–67
Douglass, Frederick, 44, 45, 81, 115–16,
    154–55, 166–67
dueling, 116–17
dysfunction, 120–21, 122–25, 126, 127–
    28, 158–59

education, 53–54, 88, 89–90, 92–94, 96–
    97, 98, 99, 146, 151, 166–67
egalitarianism, 63, 110, 126–27,
    155, 166
    basic equality, 107–8
    marriage (in-)equality, 47, 70–71, 113,
        125, 130, 160, 162–63
emancipation, 16–17, 129
embeddedness, social, 16–17, 66, 128n.5,
    129–30, 159
empathy, 115–16, 120–21, 126, 129–30,
    153, 154–55, 157–58, 161–62
engagement, 85–86, 107–8
    affective engagement, 68, 104, 143–44,
        147, 151–52
    mutual engagement, 44, 47–50, 70–71,
        153–54, 156, 166–67
enlightenment, 55, 113, 116
epistemology, 17–18, 104, 121–22, 126,
    142, 143
equality. See egalitarianism
ethnology, 92–93, 141–42
evolution, 18n.9, 50–52, 55, 81, 129
    cultural evolution, 53–54, 61–62, 65
exclusion, 30, 33–40, 56, 58–60, 66–67,
    70, 121, 123–24, 126–27, 133–34
exemplars, moral, 53–54
    moral virtuosi, 129–30
expansion, social, 13, 18–19, 23, 46–47,
    48, 59, 70–71, 73–74, 80, 92–93,
    149, 159–60
experimentation, 26, 68–72, 92–93, 97–
    98, 151, 153–54, 162–63, 166–67
    thought experiments, 58–59, 79
expertise, moral, 81, 106
explication, Carnapian notion of,
    20–21n.13
exploitation, 24n.15, 126

failure, moral, 29–30, 31–32, 47–48, 69,
    71, 77, 99, 126–27, 148, 154–55. See
    also ur-problem
    altruism failure, 127
feelings, moral, 16n.6, 20–21, 28, 62–63,
    122–23, 125, 154
feminism, 48–49, 59, 80, 104, 109–10, 134
    radical feminism, 58–59
first-order normative theory, 108–9

foot-binding, 116–17
Foucault, Michel, 163
fragility, 50–52, 149–50
framework, moral, 23, 34, 35–36, 92, 129–30, 161, 166
freedom, 67, 112. *See also* autonomy
Fricker, Miranda, 127–28
Fry, Elizabeth, 35
functionalism, normative, 123–24, 132–33
fundamentalism, 112
future generations, 86–87

gang culture, 117–18, 156
gay. *See* LGBTQ
gender, 86, 112, 126, 130, 131. *See also* LGBTQ
guidance, moral, 57–58, 90, 94, 95–96, 133

habits, moral, 82–98, 126, 133, 147, 152–53, 160
hedonism, 64–65, 99–100
Hegel, G.W.F., 112, 116–17, 133–34, 135–36, 157–58, 161
hermeneutics, 104, 105, 127–28, 143–44
heroism, 44, 63–64, 126n.4
homo sapiens, 50–51, 147–48
homophobia, 47, 123–24, 129–30
homosexuality. *See* LGBTQ
Honneth, Axel, 71–72n.46, 157–58, 163n.18
honor, 94, 116–18, 156–57
human project, 65

ignorance, 26, 41, 113–15, 120–21, 127, 155
imagination, 46–47, 92–93, 98
immigrants, 85–86, 107–8, 147
impact, social, 35–36, 60–61, 68–69, 99, 122–23, 161–62
inclusion, 36, 37, 38, 48, 56, 60–61, 75, 92–93, 134–35, 145–46, 161–62. *See also* exclusion
incommensurability, 22–24
incompleteness, moral, 85, 149–50
indifference, 30–31, 51
indigenous peoples, 24n.15, 41–43
individualism, 57–59, 64–65, 128, 157–58, 159, 161–62
industrial revolution, 35n.23
inequality. *See* egalitarianism

information, 35–36, 37, 39, 53, 74, 81–82, 91, 114–16, 152–53
institutionalism, 80–81, 97, 159–60, 161, 166
  institutional fit, 160–61, 163
  institutional friction, 160–61, 163
Instrumentalism, Antirealist, 143
investigation, moral, 36, 55, 90
isolation, social, 66

James, William, 21, 29–30, 144
Jefferson, Thomas, 41–43, 154
justice, 123–24, 168
  (structural) injustice, 33–34, 106–7, 109–10
justification, 34, 36, 39, 59, 67, 79, 87, 88–90, 122

language, 53, 86, 94, 95–96, 114–15, 154
lapses, moral, 29, 55, 83
law, moral, 53–54, 57–58, 112
lesbian. *See* LGBTQ
lex talionis, 13n.1, 55
LGBTQ, 16–17
  gay, 23, 47–48, 106–7, 112, 113, 133–34, 149–50
  homosexual, 28, 33, 48–49, 74–75, 86, 121
  lesbian, 16–17, 47
  transgender, 86
liberation movement, 48. *See also* feminism
Locke, John, 168
lore, moral, 95–96
luck, moral, 14, 105, 134, 161–62

marginalization, 30, 33–34, 35–36, 59, 109–10, 149–50, 152, 154–55
marriage, forced, 156. *See also* egalitarianism
  (sexual) obedience, 130
Marx, Karl, 127–28, 134, 157–58, 161, 163
materialism, 119, 132
Mather, Cotton, 41–43, 114–15, 152–53, 157
maxims. *See* methodology
mediation, 98
Mendel, Gregor Johann, 18–19, 104, 143

metaethics, 104, 105, 108–9, 120, 139–40, 145–46, 147, 149

*meta*methodology, 76

metaphysics, moral, 19–20, 108–9, 145–46, 149

methodology
  methodological maxims, 33–40, 47–48, 67, 71–72, 91, 97
  methodological naturalism, 106

#MeToo, 113

Mill, J.S., 64nn.36–37, 66, 68, 70–71, 111

mind-body problem, 97n.15

misogyny, 123–24, 129

movements, social, 14n.2, 44, 46–48, 58–59, 69, 85–86, 109–10, 112, 113, 117–18, 126n.4, 131, 133–34

multidimensionality, 91n.12, 92–93, 95

mutation, 149–50

Nagel, Thomas, 15n.5, 18n.8, 19–20, 75, 140, 142–44

nationalism, 150–51
  white nationalism, 107–8, 147

native Americans, 152

Nietzsche, Friedrich, 163

noncognitivism, 16n.6, 113–14, 140. *See also* cognitivism; metaethics

nonhuman animals, 34n.21, 35–36

nonideal theory, 108–9

normalization, 23, 47–48n.12, 129–30

objectivism, 26–27, 125, 140, 158–59
  qualified objectivism, 123, 125

ontology, 106, 112, 140, 142, 143, 145–46, 149
  social ontology, 128

oppression, 29, 74, 104–5, 154–55

optimism, 14, 165–66
  strong optimism, 165–66
  weak optimism, 165, 166

option-comparative, 24

option-complete, 24

organization, social, 94–96, 97–98

Paleolithic, 13n.1, 51–52, 56

Parfit, Derek, 18n.8, 19–20, 75, 140, 142

patriarchy, 48–49, 104, 109–10, 124, 126. *See also* feminism

Peirce, C.S., 73, 75, 77, 158

pessimism, 163–64, 165–66, 168
  strong pessimism, 165
  weak pessimism, 165

physics, 23, 69–70, 71–72

Plato, 49, 57–58, 112
  Platonic form, 24–25

power, 81, 109–10, 111–18, 120–21, 126–28, 146–47, 164–68
  power asymmetries, 139, 148

practice, two-component account of moral, 82–83

prejudice, 14, 29, 41–43, 86, 149–50, 166–67

problems, moral, 25–26, 28, 100, 107, 129. *See also* John Dewey
  cumulative account of problem-solving, 135–36
  procedural approach, 98, 105, 107–8, 135

productivity, 99–100, 151, 157, 160–61

prophets, moral, 104

project, moral, 49–50, 53, 54–58, 60–63, 73–74, 148, 149, 153–54, 156–57

propaganda, 114–15

protest, 13–14, 33, 41–43, 47, 48–49, 59, 66–67, 103, 109–10

protestantism, 45, 152–53

psychology, 16, 17–20, 49–59, 75, 80, 81, 87, 89–90, 92, 141, 147–48, 150–51

punishment, 33, 53–54

puritanism, 42n.2, 152–53, 157

Quakers, 13–14, 43, 45, 152

quietism, 133–34, 150

race, 13–14, 19–20, 41–43
  racism, 14, 80–81, 116, 117, 126–27, 150–51

rape, marital, 130, 159–60, 161

rationality, social, 136

Rawls, John, 37–38n.24, 54–55n.26, 64n.36, 66n.41, 108–9

realism, moral, 17–20, 106, 142, 143–46

recognition, 23, 33, 62–63, 65, 112

reflection, moral, 43, 45, 57–58, 63–64, 65–66, 67, 68–69, 81, 82, 87–88, 90, 92–93, 95–96, 103

reform, 14, 35, 70–71, 80–81, 95–98, 133–34, 146, 151, 166, 168
regress, moral, 83–84, 111–18, 160–61
relations of fit, 131, 134
relationships, human, 62–63, 130
relativism, moral, 17, 20
resentment, 14, 33, 116
resistance, 46–47, 85–86, 109–10, 164–65
responsiveness, 50–52, 61–62, 73–74, 147–48, 153–55
revolution, moral, 14, 45–46, 47, 48, 59–60, 70–71, 74–75, 106–7, 116–17

sacrifice, 13–14, 46–47, 126n.4
sanctions, internal, 53–54
Scanlon, T.M., 18n.8, 19–20, 37–38n.24, 75, 140, 142–44
scrutiny, public, 56–57, 96–97
secularism, 57–58
seeing, moral, 106–7, 146–47
seers, moral, 144
segregation, 112–13
self, social, 63–64
   ideals of the self, 65–67, 68–70, 71–72, 99–100, 146, 151, 159–60, 161
self-development, 60–61
self-understanding, 123, 128n.5
sensitivity, 87, 90, 91, 104–5, 120–21, 146
   formational sensitivity, 89–90
   observational sensitivity, 89–90
sexism, 14, 126–27, 129–30
shame, 88–89, 116–18
skepticism, 20, 22, 104, 106
stability, 62–63, 77, 78, 158–59
stakeholders, 37, 38, 107–8
status quo, 13–14, 28–29, 39, 98
stereotypes, 13–14, 16–17, 41–44, 46–47, 114–15, 149–51, 154–56
stigmatization, 151
Stonewall Inn, 13–14, 45–48
strength of will, 83–84, 91
structures, social, 16–17, 126–28, 161, 163–64
struggles, social, 120–21, 134
subjectivism, 26–27, 121–23, 158, 161–62
   qualified subjectivism, 122, 125
success, moral, 31–32, 53–54, 62–63, 69, 77, 134

suffering, 29, 35–36, 41–43, 67, 68–69, 70, 79, 86–87, 100, 123, 125, 146, 152, 153–54, 158–59, 161–62, 163–64, 166
superstructure, 74
sustainability, 167
sympathy, 29, 30, 33–34, 35–36, 37, 39, 41, 44, 47, 48, 59, 85, 86, 99, 107–9, 113–14, 152, 153–54, 155–57, 164
systems, 21–23, 24n.15, 80

Taylor, Harriet, 68–69, 70–71, 111
technology, social, 52
teleology, 24–25, 76, 119, 120, 134–35, 136, 140, 145–46
thought experiments, 58–59, 79
tolerance, 14
traditionalism, 59–60
transformation, 131, 132, 133–34, 135, 136
transgender. See LGBTQ
truth, moral, 15–26, 73–79, 103–8, 113–14, 139–49

unanimity, 27, 36, 80–81, 155
universalizability, 28, 58–59
ur-problem, 49–50, 52, 56
urgency, 34, 35–36, 67, 107, 129–30

violence, 53, 74, 109–10, 127, 164–65, 166
   domestic violence, 130
virtues, 89–90, 104–5
"virtuous spiral," 32
vulnerability, 74, 115–16, 153

war, 14n.2, 94–95, 109–10, 117, 131, 160. See also American Civil War; "woke," 117–18, 157
World War II
Wilde, Oscar, 45–46, 58–59, 133–34, 161
Williams, Bernard, 54–55n.26, 60n.30, 61–62, 64n.36, 87
women's rights, 18–19, 48. See also feminism
Woolman, John, 19–20, 43, 44–45, 81, 90, 104, 114, 142–43, 144, 152
World War II, 131. See also war

xenophobia, 150–51